101 Things NOT to Do Before You Die

101 Things NOT to Do Before You Die

Robert W. Harris

THOMAS DUNNE BOOKS

NEW YORK

THOMAS DUNNE BOOKS.
An imprint of St. Martin's Press.

www.thomasdunnebooks.com
www.stmartins.com

Book design by Ellen Cipriano

Library of Congress Cataloging-in-Publication Data

Harris, Robert W., 1954–
     101 things not to do before you die / Robert W. Harris.—1st. ed.
     p. cm.
  ISBN-13: 978-0-312-35758-0
  ISBN-10: 0-312-35758-3
    1. Conduct of life—Humor.   2. American wit and humor.
I. Title.

  PN6231.C6142 H37 2007
  818'.602—dc22

                                                     2006052209

10 9 8 7 6 5 4 3 2

Acknowledgments

Thanks to everyone at Thomas Dunne Books who worked on this book, including editor John Parsley and designer Ellen Cipriano, and also to my agent, Helen Zimmermann. Special thanks to Liz Petersen for her inspiration and support.

Disclaimer

The author believes the facts in this book to be accurate, the humor to be entertaining, and the advice to be useful. However, enlightenment, amusement, and self-improvement are not guaranteed.

What this book is about

*I think it's in my basement . . . let me
go upstairs and check.*

—M. C. ESCHER

For most of us, life can become routine, even if it is rewarding and satisfying. So well-meaning people write books that are intended to motivate us to seek greater happiness in unusual activities. The guidance usually takes the form of lists of ten or fifty or a hundred things that we should attempt because they are more stimulating or enlightening than day-to-day activities. All we have to do is spread our wings and seize the day.

But, in reality, most of us are too busy and too committed to family and job to spread our wings and seize the day. We probably are not going to try bungee jumping or running with the bulls or getting close to an exploding volcano. Most of us have limited amounts of time, money, and courage, and a too-well-developed sense of self-preservation.

So how can we find greater happiness in our routine lives? Where is the guidance for the rest of us? Duh—you're reading it!

101 Things NOT to Do Before You Die is a different sort of life guide. It is based on the idea that there are plenty of situations in everyday life that present opportunities for either gratification or frustration. We simply need to learn to make the right choices, that is, the ones that create the most satisfying and meaningful experiences.

Making those choices often can be a challenge because we are led to believe that things that are widely accepted, conventional, endorsed, or praised are the best things. But they might not be the best. Our value judgments easily can be shaped by movie producers, advertisers, bureaucrats, celebrities, and charismatic "experts." So in this book I challenge conventional wisdom and self-evident truths. I encourage you to view routine situations with fresh eyes and to evaluate the options that are available to you.

In the following pages, you'll find helpful tips on nutrition, travel, communication, art appreciation, and many other topics. In some cases I suggest that you make general changes to your thinking; in others, I encourage you to make specific changes to your behavior; and in others, I'm just having fun. So learn if you choose, expand your horizons if you dare, and laugh if you must. I did, and I feel okay.

—Robert W. Harris
www.rwhstudio.com

Contents

1

Don't watch the colorized version of *It's a Wonderful Life*

Colorization—the process of adding color to black-and-white films—was invented by Wilson Markle and Brian Hunt in 1983. Since then, dozens of classic films have been "fixed" by anti–black-and-white zealots. They even colorized *Casablanca* (ironically, Humphrey Bogart's face was actually gray). Fortunately, *Citizen Kane* has escaped—at least for now.

Colorization has been referred to as "cultural vandalism" by The Writers Guild of America West. Critic Eric Mink called it a "bastardization" of film. And Gilbert Cates, then president of the Director's Guild of America, said that it ". . . is a process of dissembling the historical and artistic fabric of our landmarks." Yet many people watch these colorized movies. Don't be one of them!

Insist on the original black-and-white. If you're ever watching an old movie on TV and you suspect chromatic trickery, check your movie guide to see how the original was produced. If it was in black-and-white, don't panic. Just take your remote, open the Video menu, and drain out all of the color. Then you can watch the film as it was intended to be watched.

Other classic movies not to watch colorized

The Absent-Minded Professor
Adam's Rib
Arsenic and Old Lace
Bringing Up Baby
King Kong
The Maltese Falcon
Miracle on 34th Street
White Heat (presumably the white part remains white)
Yankee Doodle Dandy

Fun activities

Write a scathing letter to Ted Turner, a vocal proponent—and bankroller—of movie colorization.
Start an Anti-Colorization League in your neighborhood.
Protest colorization with a silent candlelight vigil.

The inventors of colorization were Canadian—still are, for all I know.
Colorization was first used in 1970 on film of the moon taken by Apollo astronauts.
Some older TV shows are also being colorized, so stay alert!

Don't try to bathe with a sliver of soap

Frugality is a virtue. Of course. Waste not, want not. When frugality improves the quality of your life, it's a good thing. But when frugality becomes an end in itself, it's time to step back and get some perspective.

Some people believe that saving fractions of pennies is worthwhile. They are excessively frugal with *everything,* even those things that cost very little—like soap. These folks, for reasons unknown to science, use a bar of soap until it becomes a paper-thin sliver about the size of a postage stamp. Only then do they indulge themselves by opening a new bar. Don't be one of them!

Accept the fact that soap is inexpensive. When a bar no longer gives a good lather, toss it, no matter what its size. And realize that your perception of soap, and every other thing you interact with in your world, affects the quality of your life. If your mind continually gets "just scraping by" messages, it will try to ensure that you just scrape by. But if it gets "enjoying life's bounty" messages, it will try to ensure that your cup is always running over. Trust me on this one.

· · ·

Napoleon Bonaparte once sent a letter to his wife in which he told her not to bathe during the two weeks that would pass before he returned home.

❧

A man often pays dear for a small frugality.
—*Ralph Waldo Emerson*

———

Fatherhood is pretending the present you love most is soap-on-a-rope.
—*Bill Cosby*

———

Wash four distinct and separate times, using lots of lather each time from individual bars of soap.
—*Howard Hughes*

Ohmigod!

If a little sliver of soap takes a short bath in warm water it can often become supple enough to conform to the contours of its big brother, the new bar that just arrived. With a little gentle pressure these two will cling together. . . . The purpose of this soap splicing is twofold. One is that it affords some respect for the pith of the piece that once was much greater. . . . And secondly, why discard something that is still useful? . . . There is the added pleasure of seeing a successful splice take hold and providing a good home for the aging, squinny sliver.

—*Raymond Weisling*
www.geocities.com/Tokyo/8908/clatter/soaps.html

Don't hunt for
the "best" parking spot

Most people buy into the conventional notion that "good" parking spots are those near a store and "bad" ones are those farther away. So when they go to the mall, they drive up and down the lanes, desperately hoping that someone will pull out of a good spot. If, after five or ten minutes, it finally happens, the adrenaline surges. Then they drive like maniacs to beat the other shoppers to the coveted spot.

This irrational behavior has profound effects on psychological health. When these people get a good spot, they feel like a million bucks. When they don't, they grumble and complain and swear under their breath at the lucky jerks who did. They let fate determine their mood. Don't be one of them!

Always park far away from the store you are patronizing. You can do it if you simply reorganize your thinking. Just tell yourself that the close-in parking spots are the bad ones and the distant ones are the good ones. The energy you now devote to tracking down parking spots can then be channeled into more productive activities.

Reasons not to park close to a store

Walking is good exercise.

You're less likely to get dings on your doors.

The anticipation of encountering items on sale has longer to build.

You'll save gas and therefore spew less pollution into the air and therefore get to think of yourself as a more responsible passenger on Mother Earth than your fellow shoppers.

Fun activities

Mentally note the number of instances of parking rage that occur between your car and the store.

When you leave the store, point and silently mouth, "I'm leaving," to someone waiting for a spot and see how long they follow you.

The difference between a "good" spot and a "bad" one at Wal-Mart is typically around 150 feet.

Parking spaces vary in size, but usually are eight to nine feet wide.

Leon James, author of *Road Rage and Aggressive Driving,* says research shows that people who know someone is waiting for their spot will take several seconds longer to pull out just to "reassert their freedom."

I used to work in a fire hydrant factory. You couldn't park anywhere near the place.

—*Steven Wright*

Don't eat snails,
even when called "escargot"

When you were young and precocious, your parents probably insisted on your eating healthy things like broccoli. And you knew that, although it was icky, it was probably good for you. You were the kid. They were the grown-ups. It all made perfect sense.

Sadly, some people carry this childlike trust and innocence into adulthood. So when parent-substitutes, such as gourmets or other "experts," encourage us to eat icky things, these people turn off the critical part of their brain. They start nodding and convince themselves that they've really been missing something. So they decide that they simply must try the latest delicacy. Don't be one of them!

When something is clearly disgusting, keep your distance. Don't eat it, no matter what kind of fancy name it has been given or what benefits are promised. So what if somebody says it's great? Use your common sense and avoid what will probably be an unpleasant experience (even if you're lucky enough not to get sick).

Other disgusting things not to eat

steak tartar (raw beef to which a raw egg is added)
sushi (raw fish)
fugu, or blowfish (when cooked improperly, it is deadly)
organ meats (super high in cholesterol)
goat's eyes
bull's "private parts" (aka Rocky Mountain Oysters)
fried insects
scrapple (a gelatinous, gray, repulsive mass composed of
    assorted pig parts)
boiled okra (green and slimy, a hideous combination)
rice cakes (nature's version of Styrofoam)

Fugu kills 70 to 100 people a year in Japan.
Hepatitis A can be transmitted by eating raw shellfish harvested
    from contaminated waters.
Salmonella bacteria frequently contaminate unpasteurized milk
    as well as raw poultry, meat, and eggs.

"Escargot" is French for "fat crawling bag of phlegm."
—*Dave Barry*

———————

In Mexico we have a word for sushi: Bait.
—*José Simon*

5

Don't run with the bulls in Pamplona

Each July 7 the festival of San Fermín begins in the town of Pamplona in north central Spain. For the next nine days, locals and tourists party hard. There's dancing and music and lots of fun activities. Alcoholic beverages are, I hear, consumed in great quantities.

But one part of the festival is most famous: *El Encierro,* or the running of the bulls. This event involves large, disgruntled bulls sauntering through some narrow cobblestone streets on their way to the bullring. The problem is that the bulls are not alone. Courageous (trans.: foolhardy and presumably drunk) young people, wearing only white outfits and red handkerchiefs to protect their soft flesh, voluntarily run with the bulls through the streets. Don't be one of them!

Don't risk life and limb just so you can list this crazy activity on your personal "résumé." The bulls obviously don't want people to run with them, so use your common sense and just stay away. If you really feel the need to run with animals, try running with pigs or turkeys or puppies. You'll be glad you did.

∽

Pamplona is the capital of the province of Navarra in north central Spain. It's about hundred miles from southwestern France.

The festival of San Fermín was glorified by Ernest Hemingway in his fabulous novel *The Sun Also Rises*.

Since 1924, fourteen people have been killed running with the bulls and more than two hundred have been injured.

The average run lasts about three minutes.

Anyone who survives a close encounter with a bull is said to have been "protected by San Fermín's cloak." Anyone who doesn't is said to have been "killed."

Words to keep in mind

terror	contusions
charging	abrasions
goring	lacerations
trampling	ambulance
maiming	hospital
bleeding	death

6

Don't try to figure out
the lyrics to "Louie, Louie"

In 1956 Richard Berry, a Los Angeles musician, wrote a little song about a Jamaican sailor who bemoans being away from his girlfriend. He called it "Louie, Louie." The song gained in popularity on the West Coast and in 1963 was recorded by two up-and-coming groups: Paul Revere and the Raiders and The Kingsmen. The Raiders' version drifted off into obscurity. But The Kingsmen's version rose to prominence and endures to this day, despite (or perhaps because of) the garbled lyrics.

A great many people find the uncertainty of the lyrics to be unsettling. So they try to determine exactly what lead singer Jack Ely is saying, often by playing the song at a faster or slower speed. Many claim to have succeeded and, more often than not, proclaim that the lyrics are lewd and lascivious. These folks are just fooling themselves. Don't be one of them!

The Kingsmen's version of "Louie, Louie" is one of the great mysteries of life, not unlike the origin of the universe and the composition of Spam. You can speculate about it, but you can never be sure. So the next time you hear the song, just relax. It's okay that some things don't yield to intellectual scrutiny.

True or false?

1. Jack Ely had strained his voice during a ninety-minute "Louie, Louie" jam at an outdoor concert the night before the recording session.
2. Ely had braces on his teeth.
3. The microphone in the studio was positioned too high, causing Ely to strain to sing into it.
4. The band members thought they were rehearsing the song; but in fact the run through was also the final recorded version.
5. Ely had heard the song only a few times before the session.

Answers
5. True
4. True
3. True
2. True
1. True

Governor Matthew Welch of Indiana had "Louie, Louie" banned from the airwaves in his state because of the "dirty" lyrics.

"Louie, Louie" entered the Billboard charts on November 30, 1963, and remained there for thirteen weeks (peaking at #2).

After a thorough investigation, the FBI declared that the lyrics to "Louie, Louie" were not obscene. It also declared that they were "unintelligible."

Don't use premium gas
when regular is appropriate

In the good old days, when we needed gas, we would drive to a "service" station where someone would come out and provide the service of filling up our tank. Today we go to a "convenience" store, where we pump our own gas for the convenience of the manager. One thing that hasn't changed, however, are the options: regular, mid-grade, and premium.

Most drivers think that the three grades of gas represent good, better, and best. Some of them, believing that their average car deserves the best gas, buy premium in the hope that it will give them premium performance. They pay the extra twenty cents per gallon with the expectation of getting the best possible power and mileage. Don't be one of them!

Realize that octane doesn't indicate how much power the gas delivers. It indicates how well the gas resists premature combustion in your car's cylinders—known as knocking. More octane makes the gas burn more slowly, making it less likely that the fuel-air mixture will ignite on its own before the spark plug fires. Some cars (only about 5 percent) have high-compression engines and require premium gas to avoid knocking (which can damage the engine). But most cars are designed to run on regular. So if yours is one of them, using premium is just a waste of money.

In high-altitude areas, octane can be slightly lower. So in many Rocky Mountain states, regular gas might be 85 octane (compared with the usual 87).

Using a higher octane than necessary doesn't increase performance, but it does increase pollution.

Using a lower octane than necessary will probably not produce knocking because modern engines contain knock sensors. If they detect premature ignition, they retard the spark to compensate and effectively reduce the cylinder pressure. The result: You save money, but you get less power and poorer mileage. And you can harm the engine over time.

> The only way premium gas can extend the life of
> [a 1991 Bonneville] . . . is if you submerged the car in it. . . .
> That'll at least keep it from rusting.
>
> —*Ray Magliozzi*

Questions to ponder

Why don't they just call the different grades A, B, and C? Or 1, 2, and 3?

Why is the difference among the grades always approximately ten cents, regardless of the price of regular?

8

Don't worry about the inconsistencies on *Gilligan's Island*

"Just sit right back and you'll hear a tale, a tale of a fateful trip. . . ." With that catchy little song begins each episode of the classic TV comedy *Gilligan's Island*. It's a funny show about seven people who get stranded on a small island and who continually try but fail to get back to civilization.

Most viewers expect only a half hour of entertainment from the show. But others aren't so easygoing. They tend to ask questions. For example, if the tour was to take just three hours, why does the Professor have all of those books? Why do the Howells have suitcases full of clothes and cash? Why can't anyone build a reliable raft? Why does the relatively flat island have steep cliffs, mountains, and the occasional volcano? The list is practically endless. While many people briefly ponder these *apparent* inconsistencies and then get on with their lives, others become obsessed with them. Don't be one of them!

Relax. Suspend your disbelief. And lower your expectations. Realize that in TV land, two and two don't have to add up to four. And realize that, no matter how strange *Gilligan's Island* gets, it's nothing compared to the bizarro world of *Green Acres*.

Better things to worry about on TV

On *I Love Lucy*, just where, exactly, is Fred Mertz's waist?

On *The Dukes of Hazzard*, how come rural Georgia looks so much like southern California?

On *Murder She Wrote*, why does Jessica sometimes wear a brooch and sometimes not?

On *Dragnet*, how does Joe Friday manage to walk without moving his arms?

Fun activities

Whenever someone mentions an inconsistency in *Gilligan's Island*, say, "Hmm—I never noticed."

Read "Here On The Island: A Scholarly Critique of the Style, Symbolism, and Sociopolitical Relevance of *Gilligan's Island*" by Lewis Napper (available on the Internet).

Build your own leg-powered washing machine out of coconut shells, bamboo, and palm fronds.

Gilligan's Island originally ran on CBS from September 26, 1964, to September 4, 1967.

Actress Jayne Mansfield was offered the role of Ginger but turned it down.

Of the ninety-eight episodes, thirty-six are in black-and-white.

Tina Louise is still bitter.

9

Don't jump to conclusions

A woman checked in at the Raleigh-Durham airport for her flight to Boston. She knew it would be an hour or so before the plane would board, so she stopped at a snack shop. There she bought a little bag of cookies and put it into her tote bag.

Janet (that's her name) found a seat in the waiting area and began reading a paperback novel. After about twenty-five pages she started to get the munchies, so she reached to the seat beside her and took a cookie from the bag. A few minutes later she noticed out of the corner of her eye that the man two seats over also took a cookie from the bag! She became uncomfortable. A few minutes later she took another cookie. And before long the man took another cookie. Soon all of the cookies were gone. She couldn't believe how rude this guy was. Some people, like Janet, tend to reach conclusions quickly. Don't be one of them!

Now, the rest of the story: When the announcement to board the plane finally came, Janet quickly got up to get away from the man. Once on the plane, she reached into her tote to get a pencil so she could get to work on a crossword puzzle. And what did she see? The bag of cookies that she had bought—still unopened. Moral: Don't jump to conclusions.

～**10**～

Don't accumulate nonfunctional pens

It should be obvious that mental health depends, in part, on having an adequate selection of pens within easy reach. A good mix of ballpoint and felt-tip pens, in a variety of colors, gives life meaning and contributes to happiness. The only problem with pens is that they eventually give out. And most of us have no trouble tossing the ones that fail to perform.

But many people can't bring themselves to get rid of pens that no longer function. They have trouble culling the weak ones from the group. So they have cups and drawers and boxes full of pens (and pencils) of every shape, brand, and color. When they need a pen, they reach for one and try it. If it doesn't write, *they put it back* and pull out another. Don't be one of them!

Don't accumulate pens that have uncertain functionality. Check your pens and let go of the ones that no longer serve you—even if it is painful. Keep only the ones that you can reach for with confidence. This way, when you feel the urge to write or draw or doodle, you can get started without needless delay and frustration.

11

Don't eat the wrong snack during a movie

Popcorn was discovered thousands, if not hundreds of years ago. Movie theaters didn't appear on the scene until the early 1900s. Nevertheless, the two intersected, and movies became associated with popcorn. It was fate. And eating popcorn while watching movies became a tradition.

But some of your fellow citizens insist on thumbing their noses at this wonderful tradition. They'll sit and watch an entire movie without eating anything. Others will munch on pretzels or candy or (gag me) rice cakes, or download heavier fare such as pizza or subs. Don't be one of them!

Pretzels and candy and pizza are all vital to good health, and they have their place. But popcorn is the only acceptable snack to consume while watching a movie, whether in a theater or in your living room. Not only is it satisfying, it's also high in fiber and low in calories (if you don't count the oil and butter).

Different types of popcorn

Movie theater (great taste, but pricey)

Microwave (most kernels pop, but loaded with sodium—plus you'll have a residue inside your microwave oven)

Stove top (you get to control the amount of butter and salt, but you'll have a pan to wash)

Jiffy Pop (lots of fun)

Cracker Jack (yummy, but it's not hot)

Popcorn [is] the sentimental good-time Charlie of American foods.
—Patricia Linden

Popcorn is the only food you can buy in a bowl, a box, a tub, or a sack.

January 19 is National Popcorn Day.

"Gourmet" popcorn costs about three times as much as generic popcorn but isn't any better (in my opinion).

Americans—movie watchers and others—eat 17 billion quarts of popcorn each year.

In the popcorn biz, kernels that don't pop always have been called "old maids."

If Orville Redenbacher were alive today, he would be very old.

Popcorn was there

In 1946 Percy Spencer of the Raytheon Corporation was experimenting with a new type of vacuum tube called a magnetron. After he noticed that the chocolate bar in his pocket had melted, he placed some popcorn kernels near the magnetron—and they popped! Raytheon realized the magnetron's potential and went on to develop the first microwave oven.

~12~

Don't push an elevator button more than twice

I recently walked up to an elevator and noticed that the call button was lit (I assumed it had been pressed by the guy standing near the button). I'm a rational person, so questions immediately came to mind. Is this guy reliable? Was it a good firm push, or a wimpy little tap? Who is he, anyway? Is he even an American citizen? Common sense dictated that I press the button a second time—properly—to ensure speedy arrival of the elevator.

Unfortunately, most people are woefully undereducated about elevator technology and rely on superstition to guide their actions. They think that they need to press the button three or four or five times to achieve the desired result. These people are deluding themselves. Don't be one of them!

Experience tells us that pushing the elevator button twice is necessary and sufficient. The second push confirms that the button has indeed already been pushed and also lets the elevator know that a knowledgeable person is now waiting. Additional pressing would just be a waste of energy. You can't change the laws of physics just because you're impatient. So don't let irrational beliefs determine your behavior. Accept the fact that elevators respond most quickly to two presses of the button. Crosswalks, however, are a different matter entirely.

How it all started

The first elevator was built for King Louis XV in 1743. Known as the "Flying Chair," the device was intended to transport the king in style between the first and second floors of his palace. The mechanism consisted of an arrangement of weights and pulleys hanging inside a chimney (one not being used, I assume). Men—most likely unhappy men—stood inside the chimney ready to raise or lower the Flying Chair at the king's command.

Elevator haiku

Elevator sign:
"In case of fire, use the stairs."
Why not use water?

It doesn't make sense:
It's called an elevator.
But it goes down, too.

When I was little, my grandfather used to make me
stand in a closet for five minutes without moving.
He said it was elevator practice.
—*Steven Wright*

⚒ 13 ⚒

Don't be impressed when
a Realtor says "crown molding"

As houses get older, they develop more and more problems. Structural problems. Plumbing problems. Electrical problems. In other words, the value of houses goes down over time as the materials and systems and fixtures deteriorate. But, as we all know, the prices of those houses go up over time.

Realtors, who want people to buy decaying houses at outrageous prices, have to convince potential buyers that the things they are seeing have great value. So they have developed their own language that paints everything in a rosy hue and plays on our strong desire for reliable, comfortable shelter. Many home shoppers, using their hearts instead of their brains, naïvely nod their heads when Realtors speak. Don't be one of them!

Learn to eliminate the emotional aspect of Realtor-talk by translating descriptive statements into factual statements. For example, "Notice the lovely crown molding" becomes "Someone bought some inexpensive molding, nailed it to the wall, and painted it." When you translate optimistic assessments of a house's features into clear language, you get a realistic impression of the true value of the house and its many parts.

Other things not to be impressed with

"good bones" (trans.: "the house is old")

"character" (trans.: "numerous unexplainable inconsistencies and potential problems")

"quiet neighborhood" (trans.: "there's no artillery range on the street")

"cozy" (trans.: "too small for more than one or two people")

"cute" (*see* "cozy")

"charming" (trans.: "things are out of date and/or high maintenance")

"corner lot" (trans.: "there's lots of traffic noise")

"vaulted ceilings" (trans.: "there's no attic space for storage")

"potential" (trans.: "you're going to be spending some serious money")

All houses have two stories: one is the seller's and the other is the buyer's.

The Devil was talking to a Realtor. "I can make you richer and more successful than any other agent in the country," he said. "Wow, what do I have to do?" the excited agent asked. The Devil smiled and said, "You just have to sign your soul over to me." The Realtor thought for a moment and then said cautiously, "What's the catch?"

~14~

Don't use a
dangerous can opener

Sealed metal cans (made of sturdy iron) were first used for food in 1812. The supplier, Englishman Peter Durand, expected people to open the cans with a hammer and chisel. A mere forty-five years later, thinner steel was used to make cans, thus creating an opportunity for someone to invent a reliable can opener. American Ezra Warner did just that.

Although can openers have been improved over the years, most still operate by cutting off the lid with a sharp blade. When can lids were soldered on, this method was necessary to open the can. But today lids are glued on, so it's no longer necessary to cut them off. But lots of folks continue to use can openers with blades. And each time they open a can, they produce a sharp metal disk that is highly incompatible with soft flesh. They also get food on the blade, creating the opportunity for bacteria to flourish. Don't be one of them!

Why use out-of-date technology when there's a better way? Get hip and buy a modern, safe can opener that cuts the *seal*, not the metal. This clever device effectively "unzips" the lid from the can. The result: no sharp edges, and no food crud buildup on the can opener. It's safe and effective. What more could you ask for in a kitchen tool?

The first electric can opener was introduced in 1931.

The shelf life for canned foods is two years or more.

The modern can opener, using a cutting wheel that rolls around the rim, was invented by William Lyman in 1870.

The can opener used by soldiers during World War II was a small (1.5 inches long) folding device called the P-38. The origin of the name is not clear.

Pull-open cans, invented by Ermal Fraze, first appeared in 1966.

Canned foods don't need preservatives, so the salt is added because the manufacturers believe you want it.

In *Everybody Loves Raymond,* episode #9903 ("The Can Opener"), everyone in the family takes sides when Ray and Debra have an argument over a newly purchased can opener.

How the hell do I know why there were Nazis?
I don't even know how the can opener works!
—*Woody Allen*

~ 15 ~

Don't try to
beat the red lights

Basic Fact of Life #274: Some of the traffic lights you encounter will be green and some will be red. Most drivers know
that the reds and the greens average out over time, so they
don't worry too much about it. And they don't take the red
lights personally. They just stop and tolerate the mild inconvenience.

But some people have gotten confused. They see getting
caught by a red light as a sign of weakness or lack of control. So
they drive recklessly, stomping the accelerator pedal to get
through the intersection before the yellow light turns red, or
through the red light before cars from the other direction start
to move. Don't be one of them!

Don't look at red lights as obstacles to your life. Change
your perception and see a red light as a welcome sight. Let
it be a signal to relax your muscles, breathe deeply, and let
go of responsibility for a minute. Once you decide to see
red lights as opportunities rather than annoyances, you'll
never again be tempted to floor it when you see a yellow
light.

Fun activities at red lights

Recall a pleasant time in college
Recite a poem
Look at the clouds
Stretch your arms, legs, and back
Sing
Say a prayer
Imagine yourself on a beach
Plan your next big success
Observe your fellow humans

The first traffic light, invented by J. P. Knight, was installed at an intersection in London in 1868. Within a year this natural-gas light exploded, injuring the policeman who was operating it.

Drivers who run red lights are responsible for more than 200,000 crashes each year, resulting in about 1,000 deaths.

According to the Insurance Institute for Highway Safety, red light runners typically are younger, less likely to use safety belts, have poorer driving records, and drive smaller and older vehicles than drivers who stop for red lights. They also are three times as likely to have had multiple speeding convictions.

A conventional traffic light uses about $1,400 worth of electricity per year.

~16~

Don't fall into
a cheese rut

Some sandwiches can be made without cheese. The peanut butter and jelly sandwich comes to mind. But most sandwiches, especially those with meat, require some kind of cheese to create a pleasing between-bread combination. But that's okay because cheese comes in so many varieties. So there's never any reason to eat a boring sandwich.

But lots of folks do eat boring sandwiches. They have become creatures of habit when it comes to sandwich making. So they don't make a conscious and informed choice about the type of cheese to use based on the particular assemblage of meat, bread, mustard, and pickle. Instead, they make an automatic choice. And it's always American or Swiss. Don't be one of them!

American and Swiss are great cheeses and have their place. But there's also Muenster, provolone, cheddar, and mozzarella—and those are just the conventional choices. Each has its own unique flavor, color, and texture. So expand your gustatory horizons by sampling different cheeses in different kinds of sandwiches. Who knows, before long you might even be bold enough to try Havarti or Gouda.

17

Don't settle for wire clothes hangers

Wire clothes hangers are cheap and functional. Now let's look at the downside. They easily become tangled in the closet. They leave dents in the shoulders of your knit shirts. Once they're bent, they can't be returned to their original shape. And if you happen to be holding one outside during a thunderstorm, you're just asking for trouble.

Nevertheless, lots of people use wire clothes hangers exclusively. That's what they've always used, and they've never considered any other option. They keep their closets filled with jangling metal hangers, some bent, some rusted, some handed down from generations past. Don't be one of them!

Wire clothes hangers are yesterday's news. Plastic hangers are where it's at in the twenty-first century. They have nice rounded sides, which means your clothes don't get dented. It's true that the plastic ones aren't much good for rainy day projects or for opening a locked car. But they do come in a variety of colors (a useful feature for those who feel the need to organize their clothes into categories and subcategories). So, to paraphrase Mr. McGuire in *The Graduate*, "I want to say two words to you. Just two words . . . plastic hangers."

∽18∽

Don't leave home unprepared

These days it is imperative that we have certain things with us when we venture outside of our homes. We need identification, so we take our driver's license. We need to lock the house and open the car, so we take our keys. And we absolutely must be able to receive calls at awkward times, so we take our cell phones.

Thus equipped, many people feel that they are prepared for any situation that might arise. But it's a false sense of confidence. Lurking out there are problems that ID cards, keys, and phones can't possibly overcome. So plenty of people are fooling themselves. Don't be one of them!

Make sure you're fully prepared by carrying a small Swiss Army Knife on your key chain. Then you will be ready for any problem you encounter. Loose thread? Snip it. Rough fingernail? File it. Spinach in the teeth? Pick it. You'll be amazed at how often you'll use it. And you'll wonder how you ever got along without it.

Features of a key-chain Swiss Army Knife

blade
scissors!
file
tweezers
toothpick

The Swiss Army Knife story (condensed)

In 1886 the Swiss Army began providing each soldier with a single-blade folding knife. It seemed adequate until 1889, when the army introduced a new rifle that could be taken apart only with a screwdriver. So a multifunction knife was created by cutler Karl Elsener in 1891 that included a screwdriver (as well as a can opener and a reamer).

True or false?

1. "Be prepared" is the motto of Victorinox, the maker of the Swiss Army Knife.
2. The term "Swiss Army Knife" was legally registered in 1897.
3. The most versatile Swiss Army Knife has 72 functions.
4. Swiss Army Knives are used by the crews of the space shuttle.

Answers

4. True.
3. True. Included are a wire stripper, pharmaceutical spatula (huh?), and gas lighter.
2. True.
1. False. "Be prepared" is the motto of the Boy Scouts.

~19~

Don't mistake commercial printing for original art

In the world of two-dimensional art, there are drawings and paintings, which are one-of-a-kind works. And then there are *prints* (for example, woodcuts), which are many-of-a-kind works. But prints are not mere copies of some original. In the case of the woodcut, each contact of the paper with the inked board, made by the artist or an associate, produces an original print—a complete embodiment of the artist's idea.

But in the commercial realm, prints are reproductions of an original. The process of offset lithography uses tiny dots of blue, red, yellow, and black to fool the eye into seeing the entire spectrum of colors. Lots of people pay good money for reproductions of art at malls or street fairs or garage sales, confident that they are buying original prints created personally by artists. Don't be one of them!

If you're going to buy a print, take a magnifying glass along. Examine the work up close (while the seller and others stare at you like you're some kind of idiot). If the image consists of little dots, it's an inexpensive reproduction, not an original print. If this is what you want, that's fine. There's nothing inherently wrong with reproductions. But if you want original art work, keep looking.

Original print techniques

Planographic: Areas of a flat metal plate or stone tablet are masked, and paint is applied to the unmasked areas. Paper is forced against the plate/tablet by a press, and the paint transfers to the paper (example: lithograph).

Serigraphic (silk screen): Areas of a tightly stretched silk screen are masked, and paint is forced through the unmasked areas, and onto the paper, with a rubber squeegee.

Relief: Portions of a plate or board are cut away, and paint is rolled onto the remaining surface area. Paper is pressed against the surface, allowing the paint to transfer to the paper (example: woodcut).

Intaglio (in-TAHL-yo) Portions of a metal plate are removed (with a stylus or acid), and paint is forced into the cut-out areas only. Paper is pressed against the surface, allowing the paint to transfer to the paper (examples: etching, aquatint).

Useless Art History Sidebar: Do you know why "would you like to see my etchings?" is a suggestive invitation? In the nineteenth century people didn't customarily frame and hang their prints but stored them flat in portfolios. So there you are, tête-à-tête, feeling the paper, smelling the ink. . . . You see where it could lead.

—*Susan Sturgill*

20

Don't let telemarketers
ruin your day

The telephone has become an indispensable part of daily life. It lets us talk with friends, family members, and colleagues to take care of personal matters and business concerns. In the right hands the phone is merely a convenient and reliable means of communication. But in the wrong hands it can become an instrument of torture.

You know what I mean. You're eating dinner or watching a favorite show or reading a good book. Then the phone rings. "Hello," you say, naïvely expecting a friend or relative. There's a pause, then a click, and then something like this: "Hello, may I speak to, uh, Mr. or Mrs., uh, [your name mispronounced]?" Vast numbers of people let themselves be sent into a tizzy by such calls. They become disoriented and give ineffective responses ranging from "I'm not interested at this time" to "G——it, not another f——phone solicitor!" Don't be one of them!

Read *Fun With Phone Solicitors: 50 Ways to Get Even!* by Robert Harris (yes, *that* Robert Harris) and learn how to turn unwanted calls into opportunities for creative fun. In its pages you'll find easy-to-use techniques that shift the irritation from you, the victim, to the caller. By mastering a few techniques, such as "The Moron Maneuver," "The Paranoia Pretense," and "The Yada-Yada Yammer," you'll be in control the next time an unsuspecting telemarketer calls.

How to reduce unwanted calls

Put your name on the National Do Not Call Registry (*see* www.donotcall.gov for details).

Write to the Direct Marketing Association and request that you be excluded from telemarketing promotions (Telephone Preference Service, Direct Marketing Association, P.O. Box 1559, Carmel, N.Y. 10512). Include your home address, phone number, and signature.

Write a letter to credit card companies, insurance companies, and others with whom you do business, and tell them not to sell or share your personal information.

The telephone was invented in 1876 by Scottish-born Alexander Graham Bell.

Don Ameche played the lead in the 1939 movie *The Alexander Graham Bell Story,* despite that fact that Bell is described as being "tall" and Ameche was only 5 feet 9 inches tall.

The first message spoken on the phone was, "Mr. Watson, come here. I want you!"

The second message spoken on the phone was, "Good evening, Mr. Bell. I'm calling to offer you a . . ."

Don't expect an egg cream to contain eggs or cream

An egg cream is a refreshing cold drink that originated in New York City soda shops about hundred years ago. It's made of milk, flavored syrup (chocolate or vanilla), and soda water. Does it contain eggs? No. Does it contain cream? No. But it's called an egg cream. That's just the way it is. Don't worry about it.

But some folks do worry about it. They find such inconsistencies annoying, frustrating, or even disturbing. They want everything in life to be neat and tidy. They want things to make sense. So when they encounter something that violates the "rules" as they see them, they start to get a little anxious. They start searching for explanations to satisfy the left side of their brains. Don't be one of them!

The world is full of inconsistencies, paradoxes, and conundrums that are beyond our understanding. Names aren't always descriptive. People aren't always predictable. Instruction manuals aren't always clear. Fast food isn't always served fast. Accept the fact that some things just aren't going to make sense. But that's really okay because both the logical and the nonsensical are threads in the same rich tapestry. We call it life.

More surprises

Grape-Nuts cereal doesn't contain grapes or nuts.

Root beer doesn't contain beer.

English muffins didn't originate in England.

Hamburgers don't contain ham.

French dressing didn't come from France.

Welsh rabbit doesn't contain rabbit.

Buffalo wings don't contain buffalo.

Pork & beans doesn't contain pork, unless you count the little
  blob of fat that's included.

Coke doesn't contain "coke" (cocaine)—but it did until 1929.

Long Island Iced Tea doesn't contain tea.

Life Savers would be of little use to someone in mortal danger.

Even more surprises

Hummingbirds don't hum.

Centipedes don't have hundred legs.

Lead pencils don't contain lead.

Chinese Checkers didn't originate in China.

A blue moon isn't blue.

Rubber cement doesn't contain cement.

~22~

Don't fear the Sunday
New York Times crossword puzzle

Each Sunday, *The New York Times* crossword puzzle pulls us in like a carnival barker: "Step right up and try yer luck. You there, you look like a smart person. . . ." It looks so benign—just a bunch of clues and a bunch of blank squares. But once the pencil is in hand, the nature of the challenge becomes clear.

For some puzzle lovers, fear of failure begins to set in before too long. After a couple of hours of brain drain, fear naturally turns to anger and frustration for these people. Their self-esteem has been damaged—again. So they end up crumpling the puzzle into a ball and creating interesting combinations of the traditional four-letter words. Don't be one of them!

Learn the unwritten rules so you can approach the puzzle with confidence. These are the basic ones: 1. "Variant" ("var.") indicates that they're making up a word. For example, "Pancake topping: var." might require "sirup." 2. A clue with an abbreviation requires an abbreviated answer. For example, "SASE part" might require "env." 3. A question mark indicates that they're being clever. For example, "Bacon piece" might require "essay" (Francis Bacon was an essayist, you see). Space does not permit me to expound on the other seventeen rules at this time.

Frequent answers

On any given week, there's a 73 percent chance that at least two
of the following answers will be required:

RLS, initials for Robert Louis Stevenson
OTT, as in Mel Ott, former slugger for the N.Y. Giants
EMO, as in Emo Philips, comedian
EMIR, a Mideastern ruler
OTO, the Indian tribe
EEE, the width of very wide shoes
AMAS or AMAT, Latin verbs
EER or EEN, poetic contractions for "ever" and "evening"
URAL, as in Ural River (or is it Aral?)

A puzzle by Arthur Wynne, appearing in the *New York World*
    on December 21, 1913, is often cited as the first crossword
    puzzle.
Crossword puzzles became very popular in the 1920s. In No-
    vember 1924, *The New York Times* declared that the cross-
    word phenomenon was causing "temporary madness."
The first *New York Times* Sunday crossword puzzle appeared on
    February 15, 1942.
Will Shortz, the current *New York Times* puzzle editor, is a sadist.

❦ 23 ❧

Don't cook
spaghetti *al dente*

Common wisdom says that spaghetti will be perfect if it is
cooked *al dente*. That's an Italian term meaning "to the tooth."
But how does that translate into cooking time? Do you boil the
pasta for three minutes? Or three minutes and eighteen seconds?
Or four minutes and seven seconds? Who knows?

Great numbers of pasta lovers try hard to achieve the magi-
cal consistency, despite the fact that there's no agreed-upon
cooking time. They become so concerned with overcooking
that they frequently err on the low side, creating semihard and
chewy spaghetti. Then they wash it down with lots of wine
while forcing a smile and making yummy sounds. Don't be one
of them!

You know in your heart that soft pasta is good pasta. So why
risk ruining your meal by undercooking it? The next time you
have spaghetti (which should be once a week, by the way), cook
it *al dente* (as you understand the term). But then continue cooking it for two or three more minutes. You'll have perfect
spaghetti *and* you'll be able to say that you cooked it *al dente*.

24

Don't lock
yourself out

If you're like me (and I know *I* am), you've had plenty of "I can't believe I did that" moments during your life—like super gluing your right thumb and index finger together in, say, 1982, for example. Most such mistakes are merely embarrassing. But others have the added feature of exceptional inconvenience. I speak of locking yourself out of your car or house.

Not only is locking yourself out frustrating and inconvenient, it also can be expensive. You have to call a locksmith or a car service and then pay for your mistake. Plus, it's very likely that it will start raining while you're waiting for your rescuer to arrive. Everyone knows how much trouble it is to get locked out of house or car. But many never do anything about it. Don't be one of them!

Don't be inconvenienced by a dumb mistake. Keep an extra car key in a little magnetic key box and hide it under your car in a hard-to-reach location. And put an extra house key in a fake rock and place it among other rocks in—you guessed it—a hard-to-reach location. Of course, you could give a key to your neighbor, but this technique is a bit impractical because it requires your neighbor to be home whenever you lock yourself out.

25

Don't listen to prognosticators

"The past is history and tomorrow's a mystery." There's a lot of wisdom in that old saying. But you won't get that impression if you listen to financial experts, technology gurus, political pundits, meteorologists, and horoscope writers. Instead, you get the idea that, because the past is known, the future can be known with relative certainty (by those with the right combination of experience, prestige, and academic degrees, of course).

Many people, fearing the unknown, want to eliminate the doubt about tomorrow and gain an edge over their fellow humans. So they eagerly listen to the latest wisdom from prognosticators and automatically adjust their behavior accordingly. Don't they know that predictions come without guarantees, and that they frequently are wrong? Of course they do. But they nevertheless rely on them to guide their decisions and actions. Don't be one of them!

Realize that the past, although the best predictor of the future, is a lousy predictor of the future. People who make predictions are trying to convince themselves, and you, that they are able to see patterns and tendencies that have escaped others. But what if they are wrong? For maximum happiness, it's best to treat predictions with a healthy skepticism.

The future isn't what it used to be.

—*Arthur C. Clarke*

Prediction Hall of Shame

[Television] won't be able to hold on to any market it captures
after the first six months. People will soon get tired of staring
at a plywood box every night.

—*Darryl F. Zanuck, 1946*

———

The battle to feed all of humanity is over. In the 1970s and 1980s
hundreds of millions of people will starve to death in spite of
any crash programs embarked upon now.

—*Paul Ehrlich, 1968*

———

The threat of a new ice age must now stand alongside nuclear war
as a likely source of wholesale death and misery for mankind.

—*Nigel Calder, 1975*

———

The [atomic] bomb will never go off. I speak as an
expert in explosives.

—*Adm. William Leahy*

———

I confess that in 1901, I said to my brother Orville that man
would not fly for fifty years. . . . Ever since, I have distrusted
myself and avoided all predictions.

—*Wilbur Wright, 1908*

———

By 1990 people will be retiring at 40 or thereabouts.

—*Christopher Evans, 1978*

❧ 26 ❧

Don't disparage Nixon more than necessary

President Eisenhower, when asked about Richard Nixon's accomplishments as his vice president, said, "Give me a week and I'll try to think of something." But as president, Nixon was a savvy, effective leader who knew how to get things done. While in office he took advantage of his position to advance the causes of world peace, freedom, product safety, and environmental protection.

But lots of your fellow citizens focus just on Nixon's mistakes. "Nixon = Watergate" is their succinct assessment of the man and his presidency. So they know little—and probably desire to know little—about the 37th president's accomplishments. They are satisfied with their narrow view of history. Don't be one of them!

Realize that Nixon, like the rest of us, is the sum of his successes and defeats, his generosity and selfishness, and his laudable and shameful behavior. We know that he chose to engage in illegal and unethical activities, and we should hold him accountable. But to trivialize his accomplishments because of his failures is absurd. So remember Watergate when it's relevant—but forget it when it's not.

What did Nixon do?

He ended the U.S. involvement in Vietnam and brought our troops home.

He dramatically improved relations with China.

He signed treaties with the Soviet Union to limit the buildup of weapons.

He created the Consumer Product Safety Commission.

He signed the bill that created an all-volunteer army.

He called for the creation of the Environmental Protection Agency.

He enabled countless colleagues, pundits, and authors to make lots of money talking and writing about Watergate.

He provided comedians and impersonators with a wealth of material.

He helped future politicians by making clear the value of wearing makeup when appearing in televised debates.

He appeared on *Rowan & Martin's Laugh-In* ("Sock it to *me?*")

. . . don't pray when it rains if you don't pray when the sun shines.

—*Richard Nixon*

A man is not finished when he is defeated.
He is finished when he quits.

—*Richard Nixon*

Solutions are not the answer.

—*Richard Nixon*

27

Don't use a
flow-restricting shower head

Beginning in 1992, The Energy Policy and Conservation Act set limits on how much water and energy could be used by fixtures and appliances. No longer could shower heads provide a luxurious volume of water. They now had to limit the flow to 2.5 gallons per minute.

Many Americans apparently are delighted that the federal government tells them how much water they can use in a given minute in the privacy of their own bathrooms. Others feel that the requirements aren't strict enough, so they take matters into their own hands. They install shower heads that allow even *less* water to flow. Others—believe it or not—install shower heads that allow them to stop the flow of water while they soap up. These people are truly disturbed. Don't be one of them!

Enjoy your morning shower without guilt. Use as much water as it takes to feel clean, awake, and satisfied. Saving water in the shower might be good for the planet, as well as your pocketbook, but it won't be good for your mental health. It's important to get your priorities straight.

Better ways to save water

Drink your scotch neat.
Steam, don't boil, vegetables.
Wash your car with collected rainwater—but only once a year.
Use sanitary wipes to clean your hands.
Replace all of your house plants with cacti.

Questions to ponder

If less water comes out of the showerhead, don't you have to stay in the shower longer?

Considering that only 10 percent of our fresh water is used by the public (81 percent is used for irrigation and cooling of power plants), why is the government so concerned about the water you use in the shower?

A ten-minute shower requires about twenty-five gallons of water (a bath requires twice as much water—but you get only half as clean).

Motel showerheads allow 0.33 gallons per minute (a guess based on personal experience).

On *Seinfeld* episode #125, "The Shower Head," Kramer installs a super-high-flow black market showerhead in response to water-saving measures taken by the building superintendent ("Low flow? I don't like the sound of *that*.").

28

Don't be intimidated by obstacles

The importance of setting goals is clear to most adults. After all, if you don't know where you're going, how will you know when you've arrived? Most of our goals are routine, such as "Be at work on time" and "Get the oil changed every five thousand miles." But we also have dreams that go beyond the routine—dreams concerning love or wealth or career or health. Whether these dreams become goals depends on how we view obstacles.

Most people avoid setting big goals because they know that big obstacles are standing in their way. They're likely to say, "I don't have the ——— to succeed at this" (insert "time," "skills," "energy," or "money"). So they never start. And, of course, they never finish. Don't be one of them!

Of course you don't have what you need. The *journey* is what gives you the things you need for success. What appear to be mountains blocking your path are really just opportunities to grow, learn, explore, meet people, and be creative. If you take advantage of those opportunities, you surely will move toward your goal—not always predictably, and not without sacrifice, and not without setbacks. It's a commitment to the *process* that prepares you for success.

Ways to deal with a mountain

Destroy it.
Tunnel through it.
Go around it.
Walk over it.
Float over it.
Tell it to move (see Matthew 17:20 for details).
Wait (maybe it won't be there tomorrow).
Get someone else to move it.

———

Ain't nothin' easy.
—*Andy Griffith as TV's* Matlock

———

Life's problems wouldn't be called "hurdles" if there weren't a way to get over them.
—*Author unknown*

———

Life is full of obstacle illusions.
—*Grant Frazier*

———

Only those who attempt the absurd will achieve the impossible.
—*M. C. Escher*

Recommended reading

Move Ahead with Possibility Thinking by Robert H. Schuller

29

Don't take a budget bus tour of Europe

Europe is the dream vacation destination for most of us. Old World charm, interesting sites, and beer served as nature intended: in pint glasses. But some people find the idea of traveling through Europe to be a bit intimidating. There's the language barrier. And the local customs. And the unfamiliar currency. And all of those foreigners!

So they turn to an escorted bus tour and leave the decisions to others. Not a bad idea, really. But lots of American travelers, eager to get a bargain, choose a budget tour: London to Brussels to Munich to Rome to Zurich to Paris to London, all in eleven days. They want to see the most and pay the least. Don't be one of them!

Budget tours are designed to show you lots of sites in a short time. Translation: You spend most of your time on the bus, stopping occasionally for lunch or a photo opportunity. You'll see the major sites, but you'll miss the fun of leisurely exploring on your own schedule. If you do take a bus tour of Europe, make sure it allows plenty of free time in the most interesting locations. Otherwise you'll find yourself lamenting again and again, "I guess we'll have to come back here some day when we have more time."

Important safety tip

In London, look left before crossing a road (duh—that's where the cars come from!).

> Bus drivers call tours with ridiculous itineraries "pajama tours." You're in the bus from 8 A.M. until after dark—so why even get dressed?
>
> —*Rick Steves*

> . . . the biggest problem facing Europe today is that everything over there is hard to pronounce.
>
> —*Dave Barry*

Fun activities

Learn to say, "Where's the toilet?" in German, French, and Italian.

Force an uncooperative French person to take your picture in front of the Eiffel Tower.

Stand in front of Big Ben and say, "You know, it really doesn't look that big."

Walk through the Louvre until you're exhausted and thoroughly sick of art.

Each day, count the number of times your bus driver comes within three inches of a bicycler.

~≈30≈~

Don't assemble absurdly difficult jigsaw puzzles

Jigsaw puzzles provide a stimulating test of visual perception and memory. And, more important, they're fun to work on. Watching a beautiful picture of mountains or boats or buildings slowly come together because of your efforts can be a satisfying experience.

Although it's hard to believe, lots of jigsaw puzzles have been designed not for pleasure but for maximum frustration. These include one-color puzzles, round puzzles, puzzles without straight borders, and puzzles with repetitive patterns that have only slight variations. Some people labor for many frustrating hours on such puzzles, even though they know that conventional puzzles are available. Don't be one of them!

Choose jigsaw puzzles that have an interesting picture and a variety of colors and shapes. Such puzzles will be challenging without being frustrating or irritating. A jigsaw puzzle shouldn't be an ultimate test of patience; it should provide a pleasant way to pass the time with family on weekends or holidays. Oh, and don't be in a hurry to finish a puzzle. There's no prize for speed.

31

Don't put too much faith in polls

Day after day, news programs report the results of opinion polls. Although the polls usually have to do with the political scene, they sometimes cover social or economic issues.

Lots of people listen with interest to poll results. These people are impressed that the polls are touted as being "scientific." And they are fascinated that their results are reported with extraordinary precision (for example, "41 percent of Americans believe . . ."). And they tend to believe that the authority figure reporting the results is objective and knowledgeable. In short, they have great confidence in opinion polls. Don't be one of them!

Realize that potential problems make polls unreliable. For example, the people writing the questions might be biased. Or the sample population might not reflect the population as a whole. Or the questions might require knowledge that some participants don't have. Or the wording of the questions might suggest "right" and "wrong" answers. Or there might be selective reporting of the results by people who want to advance a particular agenda. So the next time you hear the result of an opinion poll, be sure to take it with a grain of salt.

32

Don't eat more
than you want

At one point in the movie *A Christmas Story*, Ralphie's little brother, Randy, is playing with his food instead of eating it. He's so cute. But his mom has had enough. So she decides to use the ultimate weapon: guilt. She gives him a classic "mother" look and says, "Starving people would be *happy* to have that."

Many of us heard a similar statement at various times during childhood. And the lesson was a good one: Don't waste food (or anything else) if possible. But some people, on their way to adulthood, misinterpret the lesson to be, "If it's on your plate, you must eat it. The food, an inanimate substance, gets to dictate your behavior. You have no choice in the matter." These people, as you might expect, tend to be overweight and unhealthy. Don't be one of them!

If you happen to end up with more food on your plate than you want, don't eat it. Admit your mistake and try not to do it again. I know, it might be hard for you to "waste" the remaining morsels. But if you eat the unwanted food, and it serves only to expand your midsection, is it not being wasted?

✍

Approximately 58 million American adults are overweight.

About 300,000 deaths each year are related to poor diet and in-activity.

Obesity is a known risk factor for chronic diseases, including heart disease, diabetes, high blood pressure, and stroke.

Yo mama needs to learn portion control

Yo mama's so fat that when she steps on a scale, it says, "One at a time, please."

Yo mama's so fat that when she wears a yellow raincoat, people start yelling, "Taxi!"

Yo mama's so fat that when she sits on the beach, the Green-peace folks show up and try to tow her back into the ocean.

Yo mama's so fat that when she sits around the house, she sits *around* the house.

Yo mama's so fat that she has to iron her clothes in the driveway.

Yo mama's so fat that she had to be baptized at SeaWorld.

Yo mama's so fat that when you tell her to haul ass, she has to make two trips.

Yo mama's so fat that when she goes to a restaurant and looks at the menu, she says, "Okay."

∽33∾

Don't see the movie before reading the novel

Popular novels often are made into movies. It's not as easy as you might think because of the fundamental differences between the two. In a book you get to experience the characters' thoughts, feelings, and desires. But in a movie you get to experience only what can be seen and heard. Nevertheless, a good story often can be translated into a good screenplay.

Many who enjoy reading novels also enjoy watching movies that are based on those novels. Seeing a story come to life on the big screen can be, one might say, a novel experience. But some of these people make the mistake of seeing a movie first and then reading the book on which it is based. Don't be one of them!

If you read the book after seeing the movie, it will be impossible not to see the movie's actors and settings and props in your mind's eye. That's a shame because part of the fun of reading is that *you* get to imagine the details of the characters and settings. If much of that work already has been done for you, your reading experience will be less active and less enjoyable.

Regardless of a novel's length, the movie script based on it will
  be between 90 and 120 pages—one page for each minute of
  shooting.
If you read a paperback novel, you'll pay about two cents per
  minute for your entertainment. If you see the movie, you'll
  pay about eight cents per minute.
Almost half of all paperback novels sold are romances.
Seventy-five percent of U.S. residents attend at least one movie
  per year.

Never judge a book by its movie.

—J. W. Eagan

Types of novels

Action/adventure	Mystery
Crime	Romance
Detective	Science fiction
Erotica	Thriller
Fantasy	Western
Horror	

Types of movies

Those with Harrison Ford
Those without Harrison Ford

34

Don't worry about the changing geopolitical scene

Frank Lloyd Wright, the accomplished architect, had some good ideas. He also had the idea that America should be renamed Usonia. Although that never happened, lots of countries do change their names. Political and military turmoil occasionally create the desire for a new national identity, and the atlases and globes have to be updated.

Lots of folks worry about all of the name changes and feel that they need to stay current. So they spend time memorizing the names of the new Soviet republics. And they learn the new names for places like Basutoland and Rwanda. And they update their world atlas at least once a year. Don't be one of them!

There's no need to devote significant amounts of your cognitive capacity to keeping up with all of the name changes in the far corners of the globe. If some change is really important, you'll hear about it in the news—like when East and West Germany merged. You did hear about that, didn't you?

All you need to know

When someone mentions Burma, raise your eyebrows and say,
  "I think you mean Myanmar."
When someone makes a comment about Sri Lanka, smile and
  say, "I always liked the name Ceylon better."
When you hear news about any country ending with "-stan,"
  furrow your brow and nod.

Best country names that never should have been changed:
  Abyssinia, Formosa, Mesopotamia, Persia, Siam, Zanzibar.
Country name with the most possible pronunciations: Qatar.
Coolest country name: Chad.
Least creative country name change: Urundi became Burundi.
Strangest country name meaning: Macedonia is Spanish for
  "fruit salad."

Make geography a part of your life.

—*advice given at www.nationalgeographic.com/geosurvey/*

35

Don't buy
fake-wood furniture

At a fateful moment in the past, some enterprising person had a thought: Instead of using pieces of wood to make furniture, why not pulverize the wood, glue it back together in the shape of a board, and cover it with a laminate that has a fake wood grain printed on it? As with most bad ideas, this one caught on immediately. Wood, a natural material that has a comfortable look and feel, began to be replaced with fake wood. The particleboard revolution was underway.

Young people, because of insufficient funds and indifference, often buy vinyl-covered particleboard "furniture" without even considering what it actually is. If X-Mart sells it, that's what they buy. When you're starting out, that's fine. But adults deserve better. They deserve real wood furniture. Unfortunately, many adults don't know that they deserve better and apparently don't care. They haven't learned to be discerning consumers, and thus they continue to buy fake-wood furniture without hesitation. Don't be one of them!

No half-natural/half-unnatural product can match the warmth and visual interest of wood. So insist on real wood furniture (if not solid wood, at least real wood veneer). The cost will be greater, but it will be worth it. But how can you be sure it's wood? When in doubt, push your thumbnail into the surface. If you can make a little dent, it's wood. If you can't, it's probably not.

∽

German wood scientist Wilhelm Klauditz invented the first particleboard in the 1950s.

My Google search for *particleboard crap* returned 19,400 hits.

As of this writing, artist Christo has not used particleboard in any of his "installations."

Coffins made of particleboard are available for the budget minded.

According to the Idaho Wheat Commission, sales of particleboard made from wheat waste are on the increase.

The Swedish word for *"particleboard"* is *spånplatta* (good to know if you're shopping at IKEA).

∽

"Last week, I went to a furniture store to look for a decaffeinated coffee table. They couldn't help me."

—Steven Wright

≈36≈

Don't spend
your loose change

Merchants, in an effort to make you think you're getting a bargain, frequently price items right below a dollar mark. For example, instead of charging you $2.00 for an item, they will charge $1.98, or $1.95, or $1.99. The difference between "1" and "2" is significant, so unconsciously you feel satisfied because you got a good price. Isn't psychology wonderful?

The problem with this system is that you end up with change—unsanitary, heavy, noisy change—after each purchase. Some of the change ends up behind sofa cushions, but the rest requires our attention. Some people really don't like having loose change and get rid of it as quickly as possible. They find it annoying and spend it at the first opportunity. Don't be one of them!

Don't be in a hurry to spend your change. Instead, toss it into a container. Over time, the container will fill up, and your loose change will add up to real money. When you finally empty the container and roll the coins, you'll be surprised at how much has accumulated (especially if you've saved quarters). You'll have enough to buy yourself, or someone else, a special treat.

Advanced technique

After you've become an expert change saver, try tossing in a dollar bill every now and then.

The approximate life span of a circulating coin is twenty-five to thirty years.

On the penny, the president (Lincoln) faces right; but on all other coins, the presidents face left.

All American coins are required to include "Liberty," "United States of America," "E Pluribus Unum," and "In God We Trust."

About half of the coins produced are pennies.

In the past, U.S. coins were at times produced in the following denominations: half-cent, two-cent, three-cent, 20-cent, $2.50, $3.00, $4.00, $5.00, $10.00, and $20.00.

Q and A

Q: Why don't ducks carry change?
A: Because they don't need it—they've got bills.

Change is inevitable—except from a vending machine.
—Robert C. Gallagher

37

Don't think of Paul Winchell as just a ventriloquist

At an early age, Paul Winchell, inspired by Edgar Bergan, decided to become a ventriloquist. And he did just that, even though it meant overcoming a stuttering problem and parental disapproval. During the 1950s and 1960s he appeared on his own popular TV shows and occasionally on *The Ed Sullivan Show*. His dummy sidekicks, Jerry Mahoney and Knucklehead Smiff, helped out, despite their often wooden performances.

Most people, when asked who Paul Winchell was, probably would say "a ventriloquist." These people are severely underinformed about a creative and talented man. Don't be one of them!

Be aware that Paul Winchell was the original patent holder for the artificial heart. He also patented a variety of other useful items, including a flameless cigarette lighter, battery-heated gloves, a portable blood plasma defroster, a freezer interrupt indicator (so people would know if their food went bad during a power outage), and an invisible garter belt. He also did the voices for Tigger, Gargamel (enemy of the Smurfs), and many other characters. And, in his spare time, he dabbled in acupuncture and hypnosis. Quite a guy.

∼38∼

Don't be a
passive spectator

Televised sports. Sofa. Remote control. These are the elements that have made modern spectating possible. Now, without leaving our homes, we can enjoy athletic competition of every kind. What's the attraction? For most of us, it's the fun that comes from cheering on our team and celebrating its skills while grumbling at the opposing team's good luck.

But some individuals actually sit and watch a football game or tennis match or golf tournament without rooting for anyone. These people aren't willing to risk the possible disappointment of picking the loser, so they give up the possible joy that would accompany picking the winner. They live in the twilight zone of neutrality. Don't be one of them!

When you're watching two teams, always pick one to pull for. Cheer and boo. Laugh and cry. Eat and drink. And experience not just the game, but the *competition*. Sure, your team might lose. But then again, your team might win. Either way, your spectator experience will have been a fun one, and you will have avoided being merely a passive observer.

39

Don't let a dead car battery inconvenience you

You probably know the feeling. You get into your car, turn the key, and all you hear is this weak little whimpering sound. Your battery is dead. Kaput. Finito. You're not going anywhere, my friend. You utter the required profanity and then proceed to the task of getting someone to help you solve your problem.

Many drivers wander around with their jumper cables, asking complete strangers if they will jump-start the dead battery. Others call a friend—a good friend—or an emergency car service. These folks know how inconvenient a dead battery can be, and yet they make no effort to be prepared to deal with it quickly and efficiently. Don't be one of them!

Buy a rechargeable emergency starter and keep it in your trunk. This inexpensive device (around thirty dollars) is half the size of a briefcase and weighs about five pounds. When your battery dies, you can use it to start your car in seconds. No hassle. For those who don't want to raise the hood and aren't in a big hurry, an alternative is a one-use starter that plugs into the cigarette lighter. It takes about five minutes to git 'er done this way.

Q and A

Q: Why do car batteries die?
A: It's a natural part of their life.

Q: Why don't batteries die at convenient times—like when you're leaving an auto parts store?
A: Nobody knows.

Q: How long are the average jumper cables?
A: Long enough—until you try to use them, at which time they automatically adjust so they are slightly too short to reach from your dead battery to a good battery.

That's why they call it the blues

How come I always lose?
My car has blown a fuse,
Oh yeah.
I got hydraulic fluid leakin' in my shoes
And the dead car battery blues.

—*Weird Al Yankovic,*
"Dead Car Battery Blues"

~40~

Don't expect all art to be pretty

Art is not meant to convey facts—we have words for that. Art is meant to convey ideas and emotions. So a painting might delight or sadden. A drawing might inspire or irritate. A lithograph might persuade or anger. Art provides an opportunity for observers to have an aesthetic experience that is primarily emotional and nonverbal.

But many folks don't allow themselves to grasp art intuitively. They simply focus on whether art is pleasing to look at. Does it consist of recognizable images assembled in a familiar way? If it does, they believe that the artist is talented and that their time viewing it has been well spent. But if it doesn't, they feel cheated. Their favorite thing to say about a work of art is: "What is it?" Don't be one of them!

By all means, you should evaluate art critically. After all, not all artists are talented, and not all art has value. Just try not to evaluate it based on how pretty, familiar, or comfortable it is. Keep in mind that artists (and composers and playwrights and architects) tend to want to "push the envelope." They are driven to translate personal visions into creative works that others can experience. So ignoring what's not pretty could mean you'll miss out on some interesting insights, ideas, and feelings.

Beauty is in the eye of the beholder

Art critics called the [Impressionist] paintings unfinished and declared the artists as madmen. In newspaper cartoons, pregnant women were warned not to enter an Impressionist art exhibition because of the danger of a miscarriage. In other caricatures, it was proposed to fend off [approaching Prussian soldiers] . . . by showing them Impressionist paintings.

—*www.artelino.com/articles/impressionism.asp*

———

Good art is not what it looks like, but what it does to us.

—*Roy Adzak*

———

An artist is someone who produces things that people don't need to have but that he—for some reason—thinks it would be a good idea to give them.

—*Andy Warhol*

———

Art is a step from what is obvious and well-known toward what is arcane and concealed.

—*Kahlil Gibran*

———

Are you really sure that a floor can't also be a ceiling?

—*M. C. Escher*

≈41≈

Don't wait idly

Right now there are countless people across this country who are waiting. Most are in a post office, while others are in a doctor's office or a supermarket. And many of them probably are staring vacantly. Is it because they are zombies? No, it is because they are waiting. And waiting, without something creative or interesting to do, is mind numbing.

Surely these folks know from experience that waiting idly is unpleasant. Yet day after day, year after year, they continue to enter into waiting situations without the slightest intention of engaging their minds. They've conditioned themselves to be satisfied with doing nothing while waiting. Don't be one of them!

Instead, be active while waiting. Plan ahead for those inevitable times when you will be forced to wait. If you're going into a likely waiting situation, be sure to carry a book or puzzle or notebook with you. And for those unexpected waiting situations, keep some stimulating material in your wallet or purse. For example, you could have a list of favorite quotations, or some verses of scripture, or a few foreign phrases. And when someone glibly says, "Sorry you had to wait," you can reply, "I wasn't waiting. I was ——ing."

Fun things to do while waiting

Work a crossword puzzle
Read
Write a letter
Daydream
Doodle
Plan something big
Solve a problem
Make a decision
Create a limerick
Contemplate a divisive issue
Recall a pleasant experience

An idle brain is the devil's workshop.
—*English proverb*

Expect poison from the standing water.
—*William Blake*

Why don't they have waiters in waiting rooms?
—*George Carlin*

~42~

Don't make tuna salad
with mayonnaise

Tuna is one of the best foods you can put into your stomach. It's inexpensive, high in protein and omega-3 fatty acids, and low in fat and calories. And it's versatile. There's tuna casserole, tuna chowder, tuna kebobs, and even tuna tacos. But without question the king of tuna configurations is the tuna sandwich (aka the tuna fish sandwich).

Most tuna eaters don't just dump tuna directly from the can to make a sandwich. Instead, they first make tuna salad. And, very likely, they make it with mayonnaise. They saw it made with mayonnaise when they were young, and so they automatically make it that way now. Don't be one of them!

Give your taste buds a treat and make your tuna salad with—are you ready?—Thousand Island dressing instead of mayonnaise. You'll be surprised at what you've been missing. And while you're at it, be sure to add finely chopped celery, freshly ground pepper, and chopped hard-boiled eggs (whites only—don't want that cholesterol to go up).

Japan and the United States are the largest consumers of tuna,
   together using two-thirds of the world's catch.

Americans eat about one billion pounds of tuna annually.

The first person to can tuna, at the time (1903) considered to be
   a "nuisance fish," was Albert Halfhill of California.

Charlie the Tuna, the spokesfish for StarKist Tuna, made his
   first appearance in a TV commercial in 1961.

In 1979 a bluefin tuna was caught off the coast of Nova Scotia
   that weighed 1,496 pounds.

According to the United States Tuna Foundation, which apparently has conducted an extraordinarily precise survey, 52
   percent of canned tuna is used in sandwiches.

Q and A

Q: Why did the tuna swim to Hollywood?
A: Because it wanted to be a starfish.

**When traveling through Kansas always carry a can of tuna fish. If
you get lost, not only can you eat it but you can stand on the can
and see Nebraska.**

—Tim Jackson

43

Don't forget who the real Batman is

On Wednesday, January 12, 1966, *Batman* premiered on ABC. The twice-a-week action/comedy starred Adam West as the Caped Crusader, who protected Gotham City from master criminals without ever parking illegally or being rude to Aunt Harriet. Although the show was entertaining in many ways—the odd camera angles, the wild colors, the hip dialogue—it was West's eccentric/droll/campy performance that made the show a success.

Some TV viewers think that Batman is just a role, and that it can be performed adequately by any actor. They probably think that Michael Keaton could dance the Batusi correctly. They probably think that Val Kilmer could say, "You *fiend!*" with the correct balance of contempt and indignation. And they probably think that George Clooney could convincingly address a citizen as "Citizen" with a straight face. Don't be one of them!

Realize that, although others might don the mask and cape, Adam West is the one and only Batman. His deadpan delivery will never be matched or improved upon. After the TV series, the role should have been called Batman—after all, there's only one Batman.

Batman, created by Bob Kane, made his first appearance in *Detective Comics* 27 (May 1939).

Adam West was born William West Anderson in Walla Walla, Washington, in 1928.

Before becoming Batman, Adam held jobs as a disc jockey, a cowboy, a truck driver, and a milkman.

Lyle Wagoner, later a regular on *The Carol Burnett Show*, tested for the role of Batman.

Adam's second wife was named Ngatokoruaimatauaia.

Quiz

Which of the following words can be used to describe Adam West as Batman?

a. smooth
b. cool
c. suave
d. debonair
e. laid back
f. so square he's hip
g. all of the above

Answer

g. all of the above.

I want to do it well enough that Batman buffs will watch re-runs in a few years and say "Watch the bit he does here, isn't that great?"

—*Adam West, aka Batman*

Don't forget what's in your freezer

Leftovers are great. It's real food, but without the hassle of preparation and cooking. But leftovers have a way of accumulating. So you put them into the freezer, knowing that a good meal will be right there when you want it. The theory is a good one. At some point you'll want to eat the rest of the meat loaf, or chicken and rice, or whatever, and all you'll need to do is take it out and nuke it.

The problem is that most people have no idea what's in their freezers. So when it's dinnertime, and they don't feel like cooking, they find themselves going through a familiar routine. They choose a container at random and examine it from several angles. Then they speculate about what it is and how long it's been in there. Don't be one of them!

Make better use of your leftovers by following two easy steps: (1) Anytime you put a container into the freezer, write the contents and the date on a little yellow Post-it note and stick it onto the container; and (2) keep a list of the leftovers on the freezer door and update it as needed. This way you'll turn chaos into order without spending too much time or effort.

45

Don't say,
"It could be worse"

We all occasionally go through times of frustration, disappointment, suffering, and pain. And it takes time to deal with the feelings in a healthy way. It's during such periods that we appreciate people who can empathize and encourage us to persevere until things improve. These folks tend to ask if there's anything they can do to help us get through the difficult time.

Unfortunately, some folks believe that what one needs when going through a difficult time is merely an attitude adjustment. One simply needs to cheer up. So they try to "help" by pointing out that things could be worse. They say exactly the wrong thing at the wrong time. Don't be one of them!

Saying "it could be worse" is counterproductive for three reasons: First, it's insensitive; it makes it clear that one's feelings aren't valid. Second, it's based on an absurd notion; there's an expectation that one will feel less pain if a more painful situation is imagined. And third, it's uncreative; it's a cliché that is used in place of authentic concern. So when someone (including yourself) is having trouble, don't focus on what could be; focus on what is.

~ 46 ~

Don't use
pointless precision

In the worlds of science and technology, precise measurement is critical to success in research, product development, and manufacturing. Scientific precision helped us get to the moon, conquer diseases, and develop electronic gizmos that are now essential for happiness.

But in everyday life, most of us don't perform experiments or design high-tech products. Instead, we work and drive and play and shop. And yet a great many people insist on using unnecessary precision. When you ask them for the time, they'll say "9:59" instead of "about 10:00." And they will tell you they have a "15.1-inch screen" on their PC instead of a "15-inch screen." And they will say that the temperature is "sixty-nine degrees," not the more reasonable "around seventy." These people have convinced themselves that tiny variations in time, distance, and other features of the world are important. Don't be one of them!

Understand that precision is crucial in scientific investigations but not in everyday life. If the difference between 9:59 and 10:00 is important to you on an average day, you might want to consider adjusting your perception. After all, you can't *sense* the difference between 9:59 and 10:00. You can't *feel* the difference between sixty-nine and seventy degrees. And you can't *see* the difference between 15 inches and 15.1 inches. So why be obsessed with such distinctions? "Close" is usually good enough. And you won't sound like a nerd.

Examples of pointless precision

A reporter gives a politician's approval rating as 50.2 percent.
A meteorologist says there's a 39 percent chance of rain.
A car dealer tells you a car has 231 horsepower.

> . . . flesh is much too uncertain and unpredictable for your scientific precision; too indecent and too terrible.
>
> —*André Brink*

> Because we can't quantify an experience, we often seem to underestimate its importance.
>
> —*Hanna Greenberg*

Advanced technique

Those who are experts at using pointless precision often will throw in the words "about" or "around" or "approximately" to sound more reasonable. For example, they might say, "Judy arrived around 2:13 this afternoon." Or they might say, "The lot is about 0.26 acres." But it's still pointless precision.

~47~

Don't try to understand the rationale behind the PED XING signs

Once upon a time bureaucrats decided that average folks needed assistance in deciding where to cross city streets. The best they could come up with was the PED XING sign. Well, they should have thought the matter through a bit more carefully. You see, if you put letters together (PED) and don't include a period, who's going to interpret it as an *abbreviation*? No one, that's who. And if you put something that looks like a letter (X) together with other letters (ING), who's going to interpret it as a *word*? No one, that's who. Everyone who sees one of those stupid signs automatically reads "ped exing," not "pedestrian crossing."

Some people go into a tizzy each time they see a PED XING sign. They speculate about why these signs exist. They wonder what kind of people would create such a thing. They lament that morons are in charge. Don't be one of them!

Instead, take a deep breath and accept the fact that, although we in America are blessed in many ways, we have crappy signage on our roads. Most signs are ugly and unimaginative, and many are downright ambiguous. Will it ever change? I don't know. I just know that it's scary to think that the best we could come up with for a pedestrian crossing sign was a silhouette of a boxy Chinese man (Pedjungyuan Xing—Ped to his friends) with a spherical head.

Designs that were rejected

PEDESTRIAN CROSSING
PED CING
P X
PEDESTR XING
PE CRO
PEDES CRING
PED XIN'

Questions to ponder

Why don't railroad crossing signs say "RAI XING?"
Why don't speed limit signs say "SPE LMIT?"
Why don't detour signs say "DET AEAD?"

A sign of the times

A person without age or sex,
With body type that does perplex.
No hands and no feet,
Standing still in the street.
This shows the PEDs where they should X.

~48~

Don't be a victim of junk mail

Wouldn't it be wonderful if all of your mail came from friends, family members, and business associates? Sure. But in reality lots of your mail comes from complete strangers who don't know you and who just want to sell you something you probably don't really want. This is junk mail, and we Americans receive almost four million tons of it every year.

Many people thoughtlessly toss their junk mail—opened or unopened—into the recycling bin or perhaps the less environmentally responsible trash can. Others go high tech and shred the unwanted material. Then they go about their lives, forgetting about the problem until the next day (not counting Sundays or holidays), when the vicious cycle continues. Don't be one of them!

Don't just stand there and be deluged with catalogs, credit card offers, and ads day after day. Take control of your junk mail problem and simplify your life. Find out who has your name and address and tell them not to sell or share your personal information with other businesses. Your junk mail will be reduced dramatically, and you'll be a much happier person.

Junk mail warning signs

It's from the "Notification Bureau."
It's from the "Regional Distribution Center."
It has apparently benefited from "Rush Processing."
It includes instructions to the post office (for example,
    "Postmaster: Deliver according to postal regulation 45.2-A").
It's addressed to "Current Resident."
It says there's a check enclosed.

Fun activities

Refuse delivery of junk mail. If it's first class, write "Refused—
    return to sender" on it and mail it (bulk mail won't be re-
    turned to sender, so don't bother).
Call the toll-free numbers on catalogs and other bulk mailings to
    request that your name be removed from their mailing lists.
Send a letter to Mail Preference Service, Direct Marketing Asso-
    ciation, P.O. Box 643, Carmel, N.Y. 15012, and tell them to
    remove you from their mailing lists. Include your home ad-
    dress, phone number, and signature.
Call 1-888-5-OPT-OUT to be removed from mailing lists for
    preapproved credit cards.
Call your credit card companies and tell them not to sell or
    share your personal information.

49

Don't watch magic with the left side of your brain

Houdini once made an elephant disappear. Thurston levitated a woman and passed a hoop around her. Chung Ling Soo caught a speeding bullet between his teeth. Cardini produced fans of cards from the air. And more recently, David Copperfield stuffed an assistant into a box about twelve inches square. Magicians routinely perform impossible feats, and all we can do is stare with our mouths hanging open.

Sadly, many of your fellow humans are unable to enjoy magic. They have become cynical during their lives and have lost their sense of wonder. They've lost their ability to tolerate incongruities and impossibilities. So they now let logical, rational, left-brain thinking dominate. Nonverbal, playful, right-brain thinking is suppressed because it is seen as inferior. When these people watch magicians perform, they say things like, "Oh, that's just a trick," or, "She didn't really disappear," or, "There's probably a wire." Don't be one of them!

When you watch magic, turn off the left side of your brain. Forget what you know about physical laws. Become childlike and stop trying to come up with plausible (but probably wrong) explanations for what you see. You'll enjoy the show much more. And if you're relying too heavily on left-brain thinking in general, it's time to get things back into balance by giving more attention to your feelings and intuitions.

Quiz

Match the magician to his real name:

Andre Kole	Harry Bouton
Cardini	Howard Thurston
Chung Ling Soo	William Robinson
David Copperfield	Erich Weiss
Harry Blackstone, Sr.	Richard Pitchford
Harry Houdini	David Kotkin
Howard Thurston	Bob Gurtler, Jr.

Answers

Andre Kole is Bob Gurtler, Jr.
Cardini is Richard Pitchford.
Chung Ling Soo is William Robinson.
David Copperfield is David Kotkin.
Harry Blackstone, Sr., is Harry Bouton.
Harry Houdini is Erich Weiss.
Howard Thurston is Howard Thurston.

Nothing I do can't be done by a 10-year-old—with 15 years of practice.

—Harry Blackstone, Jr.

∾50∾

Don't get the
good quotes wrong

Say something about the power of the written word—something original—that's profound or clever or poignant. Oh, and make it memorable. I'll wait. *[Drumming my fingers while waiting.]* As you can see, it's not so easy to do. But others have done it (for example, "The pen is mightier than the sword"). So we often quote others who have, at some point, been profound or clever or poignant.

Most of us draw on the words of others during conversation out of habit. A number of phrases are just so well known that they often seem appropriate. The problem is that some people are careless when borrowing the words of others. Don't be one of them!

If you're going to use the sayings of celebrities, politicians, writers, or artists, try to get them right. Or, as an easy alternative, at least be aware that you're not getting them right.

Common misquotations

Franklin Roosevelt didn't say, "We have nothing to fear but fear itself." He said, "The only thing we have to fear is fear itself."

Mae West didn't say, "Why don't you come up and see me sometime." She said, "Why don't you come up sometime and see me?" (*She Done Him Wrong*, 1933).

Marie Antoinette didn't say, "Let them eat cake." She said, "Let them eat bread."

Shakespeare's Hamlet didn't say, "Alas, poor Yorick, I knew him well." He said, "Alas, poor Yorick—I knew him, Horatio" (*Hamlet* V, i).

In the Bible, Paul didn't say, "Money is the root of all evil." He said, ". . . the love of money is the root of all evil" (1 Timothy 6:10).

Quotable lines that never were spoken

"May the force be with you." Attributed to Alec Guinness in *Star Wars* (1977).

"I want to suck your blood." Attributed to Bela Lugosi in *Dracula* (1931).

"You dirty rat!" Attributed to James Cagney.

"Me Tarzan, you Jane." Attributed to Johnny Weismuller in *Tarzan, the Ape Man* (1932).

"Elementary, my dear Watson." Attributed to Arthur Conan Doyle's Sherlock Holmes.

"Beam me up, Scotty." Attributed to William Shatner in *Star Trek* (TV series).

"Play it again, Sam." Attributed to Humphrey Bogart in *Casablanca* (1942).

∽≈ 51 ≈∽

Don't create an
indestructible home

Your home is your castle. It's where the hearth is. And, according to the witch's Dorothy, it's the place unlike any other place. But on the practical side, it's a collection of building materials and furnishings. And they, as with all things that people use, show signs of wear over time. After a while, homes start to reflect the lifestyles and personalities of the family members who live there.

But many other homeowners seem obsessed with creating a home that will never show any wear. So they have granite countertops in the kitchen. And synthetic laminate cabinets in the bathrooms. And glass-and-steel furniture. And floors of concrete or marble or slate. They seem more determined to create a monument to modern building materials than a home. Don't be one of them!

Scratches are okay. Dents are okay. Scuff marks are okay. They all show that you and your family actually went about the business of living and playing and growing. If your home looks the same year after year, and shows no evidence of human activity, will it really be the best home possible?

~52~

Don't overvalue symmetry

Symmetry is defined as the "correspondence in size, shape, and relative position of parts on opposite sides of a dividing line or median plane or about a center or axis." It's an attempt to create a pleasing or balanced arrangement by following a relatively rigid methodology. The ancient Greeks absolutely adored it, as you can tell from their architecture. (Of course they did tolerate some asymmetry—just look at feta cheese.)

Even today many people believe that symmetrical arrangements are superior to asymmetrical arrangements. So when they compose a letter, or hang several pictures on a wall, or choose a business card design, they automatically go for the symmetrical look. They prefer to play it safe and stay in familiar territory. Don't be one of them!

Symmetry is, more often than not, boring. It also has a static quality. And it leaves little room for creative thought. So why rely on it exclusively? Why not take a little risk occasionally? Asymmetry has the potential for being pleasing, balanced, and organized, but in a dynamic way. So loosen up when you design or arrange or assemble. The center line might not be as important as you thought.

53

Don't read
War and Peace

Leo Tolstoy was a genius. At least that's what I've been told. So I'm sure he knew how to write concisely. Why, then, are his books so long? Was he, perhaps, overcompensating for some, er, deficiency? You don't have to be a psychiatrist to figure this one out.

Nevertheless, his *War and Peace* is a classic of literature. The Penguin edition runs 1,444 pages. Set in a different font, it might be 1,600. Or 1,512. Who knows? The point is that it's way too long. Nevertheless, lots of folks feel a compelling urge to read this book cover to cover, and happily invest twenty-five to thirty very quiet hours doing so. Don't be one of them!

Sure, *War and Peace* has a hero and a heroine, as well as plenty of romance, conflict, and bravery. And you get to learn more than you ever wanted to know about the Napoleonic Wars. But again, I come back to the "way too long" aspect. So if you really want to read a classic, try one of these:

Goldfinger by Ian Fleming
Moonraker by Ian Fleming
Live and Let Die by Ian Fleming
Diamonds are Forever by Ian Fleming

True, you won't learn much about the Napoleonic Wars, but the information about cars, sex, and guns will more than make up for that.

Other unnaturally thick books you might want to avoid

Anna Karenina by Leo Tolstoy
The Brothers Karamazov by Fyodor Dostoevsky
Atlas Shrugged by Ayn Rand
Clarissa by Samuel Richardson
The Count of Monte Christo by Alexander Dumas
Remembrances of Things Past by Marcel Proust (1,018 pages—
   and that's just volume 1—there are seven more!)

Questions to ponder

If all of the copies of *War and Peace* were laid end to end, how
   many people would care?
Which makes a better doorstop: a hardback copy of *War and
   Peace* or a paperback copy?

Tolstoy was treated for venereal disease in 1847.
Tolstoy began writing *War and Peace* in 1863 and didn't finish until 1869.
Tolstoy's wife, Sophia, bore him thirteen children. No proof ex-
   ists that they ever read *War and Peace*.

$\approx$54$\approx$

Don't get caught
in the rain

Umbrellas, in various configurations, have been in use for over three thousand years. At first they were used primarily as sun shades for royalty. But today they serve mainly to keep us all relatively dry when we're out in the rain. Are they expensive? Are they hard to find? No and no. So why, then, do so many people depend on only one umbrella to meet their rain protection needs?

You know these people. If the weather looks threatening when they leave home, they take their one umbrella with them and thus are ready in case it rains. But if the weather looks nice, they leave their umbrella at home, creating the opportunity to be inconvenienced and thoroughly drenched if the weather changes during the day. Don't be one of them!

Don't let unexpected bad weather create a problem for you. Make sure you have three umbrellas: one at home, one in the office, and one in the car. (The compact, folding ones are ideal.) This way, when rainy weather suddenly appears, you will be prepared. While others are dashing madly to their cars or offices, getting soaked, you'll be calm and dry.

"Umbrella" comes from the Latin word *umbra,* meaning "shade" or "shadow."

Umbrella availability is most important in Louisiana and Alabama, which get more than fifty-five inches of rain per year, and least important in Arizona and Nevada, which get less than one-seventh of that amount.

In 1852 Samuel Fox invented the steel-rib umbrella (whale bones were often used before this time). It provided, he thought, a practical way to use up excess stocks of stays that were used in women's corsets.

In *Seinfeld* episode #141, "The Checks," George says to Jerry, "Who buys an umbrella anyway? . . . you get 'em for free in the coffee shop in the metal cans."

Quiz

1. What rotund actor often carried an umbrella on a 1960s sitcom?
2. What arch villain of Batman's always had his umbrella with him?
3. In which movie did Gene Kelly dance with an umbrella?

Answers

3. *Singin' in the Rain* (MGM, 1952).
2. Penguin (played by Burgess Meredith).
1. Sebastian Cabot as Mr. French in *Family Affair.*

55

Don't equate "lite" with "healthy"

A great many people are concerned with maintaining good health and/or losing weight. So they automatically buy "lite" or "light" food products, believing that they are healthy choices. But in reality those terms simply mean that the calories have been reduced by a third, or that the fat has been reduced by half, relative to the original product.

What if the light product has lots of sodium, which contributes to high blood pressure and increases the risk of heart disease? What if it's full of sugar, which can contribute to osteoporosis, cancer, and diabetes? What if it contains trans fats, which clog your arteries and have a negative impact on cholesterol levels? Many people don't really care as long as they are limiting their caloric intake. Don't be one of them!

Read the nutritional labels to know if your "light" foods are really good for you. Watch out for excessive salt (anything with "sodium" in the name). Watch out for sugar (aka corn syrup, sucrose, dextrose, glucose, fructose, maltose, honey, or molasses). And watch out for trans fats (contained in shortening and hydrogenated oils). As nutritionist Adelle Davis once said, "Let's not be part-smart."

Inaccurate information was allowed on food labels until 1924.

Beginning in 1973, food labels had to give information about vitamin and mineral content.

Beginning in 1994, food labels were required to list "nutrition facts" and give information about fat, cholesterol, fiber, sugar, and other useful information.

Food labels now are required to give information about trans fats.

Lite products we'll probably never see

lite beef jerky
lite Big Mac
lite anchovies
lite corned beef hash
lite bourbon
lite Twinkies
lite aerosol cheese
lite Novocaine

Question to ponder

Why don't light products cost less than their nonlight counterparts?

Recommended reading

Let's Eat Right to Keep Fit by Adelle Davis

≈56≈

Don't solve problems by brute force

Gary L. Bertrand provides a view that is all too common: "Solving a problem is a form of combat, requiring stamina, endurance, and skill. . . ." We have been taught to think in terms of "attacking" problems and wrestling them to the ground with conscious, logical thought. An alternative view is given by Maxwell Maltz: ". . . our Creator made ample provisions for us to live successfully . . . by providing us with a built-in creative mechanism. Our trouble is that we ignore [it] . . . and try to . . . solve all our problems by conscious thought, or 'forebrain thinking.'"

Most people believe that problems yield only to conscious thinking. They think that the unconscious is too unreliable and unpredictable, so they don't trust it. When they have a problem, they strain their brains trying to find an acceptable solution through rational thought and willpower. They try to force a solution to appear. Don't be one of them!

Learn to trust your creative mechanism. After defining your problem, thinking intensely about it, and forming a deep desire for a solution, relax. At this point further worry and conscious effort won't help. Let your unconscious mind take over. Forget about the problem and move on to something else for a while. Then at some unguarded moment the solution you need will occur to you. So be ready for it.

Recommended reading

Psycho-Cybernetics by Maxwell Maltz
Think and Grow Rich by Napoleon Hill
The Universal Traveler by Don Koberg and Jim Bagnall

> I have found . . . that, if I have to write upon some rather difficult topic, the best plan is to think about it with very great intensity . . . for a few hours or days, and at the end of that time give orders, so to speak, that the work is to proceed underground. After some months I return consciously to the topic and find that the work has been done.
>
> —*Bertrand Russell*

> . . . any impulse of thought which is repeatedly passed on to the subconscious mind is, finally, accepted and acted upon by the subconscious mind, which proceeds to translate that impulse into its physical equivalent . . .
>
> —*Napoleon Hill*

> Worry is not preparation.
>
> —*Cheri Huber*

Don't buy "insurance" in blackjack

In blackjack the best hand is a "natural": an ace and a 10-value card (totaling 21). In a casino, if the dealer's face-up card is an ace, you will be offered the chance to buy *insurance* by placing another bet (half the value of your original bet). If the dealer does have a natural, your insurance bet pays 2 to 1, but you lose your original bet. So you break even—you win as much as you lose. If the dealer doesn't have a natural, you lose the insurance bet, and the hand continues (with your original bet still in play).

Lots of gamblers think that buying insurance is a good idea. They believe that it helps to minimize the possibility of losing money. Don't be one of them!

Realize that the deck is stacked, so to speak, against you. Consider the following. In a deck of cards there are, for every 13 cards, four that have a value of 10 (10, jack, queen, and king) and nine that don't. So, statistically, taking insurance will be the correct play only four times out of 13. For example, if your original bet is $10, and your insurance bet is $5, you'll win $40 because insurance pays 2 to 1 ($4 \times \$5 \times 2$)—but you'll lose $45 ($9 \times \$5$). Conclusion: Don't take insurance.

A casino conundrum

Five friends sit down to play blackjack at a table where the dealer is using only one deck of cards. After the initial deal (two cards to each player and the dealer), player 1 says, "Hit me." He looks at his cards, and again says, "Hit me." Twice more he takes a card and still has not gone over 21. At this point one of his friends gets curious and says, "Dealer, what's the maximum number of times we five players could say "Hit me" during one hand without anyone busting?" The dealer quickly figured out the answer. Can you?

Answer

If you came up with 16, don't feel bad. You're close. The answer is 17, and here's how. Player 1 gets a 2 on the deal, and gets hit with 3 4 5 6 (for a total of 21—and so do players 2, 3, and 4. Player 5 gets 7 7 on the deal, and then gets hit with 7. Total: 17 hits, and nobody busted!

Unless a shoe is rich in tens,
Insurance ain't for denizens
Of blackjack pits in gambling dens.

—*Sumner A. Ingmark*

~58~

Don't get confused about who won the most Olympic gold

The opportunity to compete in the Olympics is the dream of most young athletes. For the ones who perform at the highest level, a gold medal is their reward. And those few who excel again and again eventually accumulate multiple gold medals.

Many individuals, when asked who has won the most gold medals, will guess swimmer Mark Spitz (9). Others will think the leader is the Finnish runner Paavo Nurmi (9) or track and field star Carl Lewis (9). Don't be one of them!

Spitz and Nurmi and Lewis did have remarkable Olympic careers, each winning 9 gold medals (as did Soviet gymnast Larissa Latynina). But the record is 10 golds, won in the early twentieth century by American Ray Ewry at the Paris, Saint Louis, Athens, and London games. He dominated the standing jumps (no longer contested) and was never defeated in Olympic competition. He established remarkable world records in each: standing high jump (5'5"!), standing long jump (11'4⅝"!), and standing triple jump (34'8½"!). Pretty good hops for someone who contracted polio at an early age.

~59~

Don't give
necessities as gifts

We all need a variety of mundane items to function effectively in our daily lives. We need underwear and toasters and razors and sheets. In fact, such items are so necessary that we automatically replace them when they wear out or run out or stop working.

Many people apparently don't realize that others are capable of buying such necessities for themselves. So when it's time to buy a gift for someone, they always choose something commonplace and necessary. And, of course, when the recipient opens the gift, there's a look of disbelief/confusion/disappointment, followed by a faint, forced smile. But the givers are oblivious to the reaction and believe that they have done well. Don't be one of them!

Don't give necessities as gifts (unless they have been requested). A gift should bring a smile to the face of the recipient, and necessities are unlikely to produce that response. So the next time you buy a gift, make sure it's something that will be appreciated. After all, it's the thought that counts. And if that thought is impersonal, then the gift will be practically meaningless.

Don't write e-mails
in all caps

Some computer users—kids for the most part—write their e-mails in all lowercase letters and abbreviate simple words like "are" (r) and "you" (u). Most adults, however, adhere to standard English and writing conventions. They use uppercase and lowercase text, proper punctuation, and good grammar—or at least come close.

But certain people, in an effort to get your attention, convey importance, or be distinctive, intentionally violate convention. They write e-mails in capital letters. These people belong in the same category as red-light runners and doctors who keep you waiting. Don't be one of them!

Writing in all caps is like shouting. DO YOU KNOW WHAT I MEAN? WELL, DO YOU? Not only is it obnoxious, it's also hard to read. Caps are more blocklike and less distinctive than lowercase letters, thus making reading a challenge. And many people won't even bother. So don't get under the skin of the people you want to read your e-mails. Writing in all caps is a big no-no. Stick to conventional text.

The first e-mail was sent in late 1971 by Ray Tomlinson, an employee at BBN Technologies.

Oops

In 1968, when Senator Ted Kennedy heard that Massachusetts company BBN had won the contract to develop an "interface message processor," he sent a telegram congratulating the company for winning the "interfaith message processor" contract.

Double oops

In an interview with Wolf Blitzer, Al Gore said, "During my service in the United States Congress, I took the initiative in creating the Internet." However, Al Gore was not yet in Congress in 1969 when ARPANET (the original Internet) was developed or in 1974 when the term "Internet" came into use.

Questions to ponder

If Al Gore didn't invent the Internet, who did?
Is there any way to say "www" without sounding like a moron?
Can a person who writes "e-mail" be compatible with a person who writes "email"?

∽61∽

Don't refer to the past as "a simpler time"

Pick any decade in the past and you'll find different technology, different norms, different heroes, and different music compared to today. Things change because of innovation, societal pressures, catastrophes, optimism, and fear. Progress happens, for better or worse.

Some people look back in time and, with a knowing smile, declare it to have been "a simpler time." They apparently see life in the past as less complicated and the people as more naïve. They think that, compared to today, the problems were less challenging, the questions were more easily answered, and the pressures of daily life were less intense. Don't be one of them!

Realize that, in most ways, the past wasn't simpler. People weren't simpler: They survived hardships, worked, raised families, and planned for the future. Machines and devices may have been less sophisticated, but using them was anything but easy and simple. And problems weren't simpler: There were more unconquered diseases, more unsafe workplaces, and more social injustice. So the idea that the past was a simpler time is, quite simply, ridiculous.

A simpler time (?) one generation ago

To find out something, you had to drive to a library and search through card catalogs, microfiche records, and books.

If you were one of the few who had a personal computer, you had to communicate with it by typing commands such as XCOPY *.DOC A:.

There was no digital answering machine, Prozac, Doppler radar, or disposable contact lenses.

A simpler time (?) two generations ago

To change the TV channel, you had to get up, walk to the TV, and turn a dial.

To cook a frozen dinner, you had to preheat your oven and then cook the sucker for at least an hour.

To make a telephone call, you had to manually rotate a dial for each digit.

There was no personal computer, compact disc, Astroturf, or Liquid Paper.

A simpler time (?) three generations ago

To dry your washed clothes, you had to hang them on an outdoor clothesline for a few hours.

If you wanted to get into college, you actually had to earn good grades in high school.

There was no dialysis machine, freeze-dried coffee, Velcro, or polio vaccine.

62

Don't finish a novel if it's not entertaining

Publishers want to make money, right? Right. So they go to great pains to publish only those novels that are interesting and entertaining, right? Wrong. Publishers turn out plenty of good books, but also an amazing variety of books that are boring, poorly written, or just plain dumb. Unfortunately, it's impossible to tell from reading the book jacket whether a novel actually will be enjoyable.

Lots of people have the idea that once they begin a book, they are honor bound to finish it. It's their duty. They've made a commitment, and, by golly, they must see it through. So they spend a number of hours doing something they really don't want to do. Don't be one of them!

If you've read thirty or forty pages of a novel, and you find that you are not entertained or intrigued or interested, stop reading. So what if it's written by a famous author, or if it's on the bestseller list? It's your time you're spending, so spend it well. If it's a library book, return it and find another. If you bought it, sell it at a used bookstore. Or better yet, give it to Goodwill and take a tax deduction. There are plenty of good books out there, so stop wasting time and go find one of them.

The typical Tom Clancy novel contains more than 200,000 words.

Women outnumber men as buyers and readers of fiction.

The average adult reading speed is 200 to 250 words per minute.

Quiz

1. How old was Robert Ludlum when he began writing?
2. Who began a novel with the words, "It was a dark and stormy night . . ."?
3. How many rejections did Richard Bach get before finding a publisher for *Jonathan Livingston Seagull*?
4. How many Western novels did Zane Grey write?

Answers

4. Grey wrote 57 Western novels.

3. Bach got 18 rejections for the book.

2. Edward Bulwer-Lytton, a nineteenth-century British novelist.

1. Ludlum was 42.

My test of a good novel is dreading to begin the last chapter.

—*Thomas Helm*

✒63✒

Don't let your limitations
become excuses

Some things in life are important, and they deserve your full commitment. It's important to do your best when performing your job, cultivating your marriage, raising your children, and competing for the league bowling championship. Giving it your all is a necessary part of success, which gives us pride and joy and a sense of self-worth.

Unfortunately, at some point early in life, we all heard someone say, "Always do your best." And a lot of people accepted the wisdom of this advice without ever questioning it. These are the people who avoid trying new activities because they are afraid that someone will judge their effort and chide them if it's not their "best." So these people miss out on lots of fun, mind-expanding, enjoyable activities because of the "always do your best" mentality. Don't be one of them!

Adjust your perception. Realize that it's okay to be an average golfer if you like to play golf. And it's okay to be a mediocre artist if you enjoy painting. And it's okay to be an unexceptional pianist if playing piano makes you feel good. If there's something you enjoy, just do it and forget "their" standards. If you like doing it, concern with how well you do it and with the evaluations of others should be irrelevant.

Questions to ponder

Do you worry about "doing your best" when you walk your dog? Or when you eat breakfast? Or when you watch a movie?

I cling to my imperfection, as the very essence of my being.
—*Anatole France*

Ring the bells that still can ring
Forget your perfect offering.
There is a crack in everything,
That's how the light gets in.

—Leonard Cohen

I respect my limitations, but I don't use them as an excuse.
—*Stephen R. Donaldson*

———

Change and growth take place when a person has risked himself and dares to become involved with experimenting with his own life.
—*Herbert Otto*

64

Don't serve ham at Thanksgiving

Imagine you've just eaten turkey, stuffing, cranberries, green bean casserole, mashed potatoes, rolls, and pumpkin pie. Yummm. It's the classic Thanksgiving dinner that's preceded by anticipation, accompanied by awkward conversation, and followed by a nap. Although the side dishes may vary, turkey always should be the central part of the meal. It's tradition. If you don't believe me, just look at that Norman Rockwell painting.

Many Americans, in an attempt to convince themselves and others that they are trendy, independent, or highly evolved, turn up their noses at traditions. To them, that's "in the box" thinking that limits their spontaneity and ability to enjoy life. So at Thanksgiving, they are likely to serve ham, or pizza, or even sushi. Don't be one of them!

Traditions aren't merely habits that save us from thinking creatively and making decisions. Traditions connect us with the past, giving our lives a measure of stability and predictability. They give us emotional comfort by keeping us aware of who we are, where we came from, and what we value. So don't ignore traditions, especially on Thanksgiving. Serve turkey. Without it, there are no cold turkey sandwiches, no turkey pot pie, no turkey soup. . . .

Robert W. Harris

Turkey quiz

1. What do you call the feathers on a turkey's wings?
2. Is is possible to make a turkey float?
3. What did the mother turkey say to her disobedient children?
4. How do you keep a turkey in suspense?

Answers

4. I'll let you know next week.
3. If your father could see you now, he'd turn over in his gravy.
2. Yes. You need two scoops of ice cream, some root beer, and a turkey.
1. Turkey feathers.

For forty years, Sarah Josepha Hale wrote letters to presidents asking them to proclaim a national day of thanksgiving. President Lincoln did just that. But it wasn't until 1941 that Congress sanctioned Thanksgiving as a legal holiday that would fall on the fourth Thursday in November.

Harry Truman began the tradition of granting a presidential pardon to a selected turkey right before Thanksgiving each year. The bird, racked with guilt about his good fortune, then goes to live out his life at Kidwell Farm, a petting zoo in Herndon, Virginia.

65

Don't read the
pop-up ads on TV

A few years ago television started down a slippery slope. Thanks to digital technology, networks became able to superimpose annoying logos in a bottom corner of the screen. After some practice, we all learned how to filter them out (at least most of the time) and enjoy our favorite shows. But I knew it was a bad sign. I knew worse things were coming.

I was right, of course. Not long ago networks started flashing pop-up ads on the screen during shows. We can only imagine the network executives' decision process: "What can we do to irritate our viewers and make it difficult for them to enjoy our programs? Pop-up ads! Of course!" Some TV viewers read all of these ads. Apparently they want to be reminded about what show they are watching. And they want to have one-third of the picture obscured. And they want to lose track of what's happening in the show. Don't be one of them!

Don't validate these stupid, annoying ads by paying attention to them. When you see one start to appear on the screen, cover it with your hand. Or close your eyes for ten seconds. Your viewing experience will be much more pleasant.

66

Don't put an inane greeting on your answering machine

I think you'll agree with me when I say that the phone answering machine is one of the greatest inventions ever created. Just imagine: You're not home, and yet you can receive incoming calls from friends, family members, and bothersome telemarketers. What a deal. All you have to do is record a greeting that encourages your callers to leave a message.

Some people insist on putting really lame greetings on their machines. For example, they say something relatively unfriendly like, "You know how it works," or, "Leave a message." Or they try to be cute with something like "Here's the beep . . . no, *here* it is . . . wait, wait, *here's* the beep." Or they insist on conveying TMI* with a long-winded exposition about how hectic their lives are at the moment. Don't be one of them!

Conventional greetings are fine. If you have one on your answering machine, don't worry. No one will think less of you. But if you do decide to record a greeting that will stand out, at least make it something clever (which is not a synonym for "annoying," "offensive," "political," or "inane") so callers will admire you and want to emulate you.

*TMI: Too much information.

67

Don't play Scrabble by the conventional rules

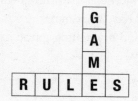

Scrabble is a fun board game that requires verbal skill, luck, and a modest level of manual dexterity. As you might know, there are three types of tiles that create opportunities for high-scoring turns: the 10-pointers (Q and Z), the 8-pointers (J and X), and the two blanks (which can be used as any letter). So if you happen to pick most of those tiles, you can basically mop the floor with your opponent. Lopsided games are a real possibility.

Most players never have given this problem much consideration. They play Scrabble by the conventional rules that are printed inside the box lid. Each time they play, they hope that they, and not their opponents, get most of the good letters and can cruise to victory. Don't be one of them!

For maximum Scrabble fun, play by the following modified rule: You and your opponent can each use only one 10-pointer, one 8-pointer, and one blank. (And because the Q requires a U to be useful, you should also split the four U's.) This variation will make your games closer and much more challenging. Luck and skill will still be required to win. But now luck will play less of a role.

❧

Scrabble, originally called Lexico and later changed to Criss-Cross Words, was created in 1931 by architect Alfred Butts.

Scrabble was first marketed in 1949.

Karl Khoshnaw, of Manchester, England, holds the record for the most points in one turn: 392 for "caziques" (of course he was playing by the conventional rules).

The Scrabble board has 225 squares.

Scrabble is the second bestselling game in U.S. history (just behind Monopoly).

Words every Scrabble player should know

qua
quai
quark
quipu
quod
xi
xu
yegg
yerk
yeuk
yogh
zax
zayin
zebu
zoa
zoon

68

Don't use Times and Helvetica fonts

Back in the Dark Ages, when personal computers and laser printers were new, only a handful of fonts were available. They included Times Roman, a serif font (with small strokes at the ends of the main strokes, as you see here) and Helvetica, a sans serif font (without serifs, as you see here). Finally, typography for the masses! It was an exciting time for those of us who had used typewriters for years and years.

At the time those fonts were adequate. But today we have hundreds of serif and sans serif fonts that are aesthetically pleasing and suitable for any type of document you might create. Many computer users, however, cling to Times and Helvetica the way Linus clings to his blanket. They automatically choose them for their printed documents without even considering the options. Don't be one of them!

Don't produce boring, mundane documents by using the same fonts over and over again. After all, type is not merely functional. In addition to conveying a message, it also gives a page a particular "look and feel." So experiment with fonts to find those that are consistent with your document's purpose, its content, the intended audience, how it will be used, and how often it will be used. Loosen up and be creative (within the bounds of good taste, of course).

The original Times font was created by Stanley Morison in 1929 for the *Times* newspaper in London (which dubbed it Times New Roman).

The original Helvetica font was developed by Max Miedinger in 1957 for the Haas Type Foundry in Switzerland.

In 1985 a slow laser printer with little memory, accommodating digital versions of Times and Helvetica, cost about $6,000. Today vastly superior models can be found for around $200.

Alastair Johnston makes an analogy between
the spread of Helvetica and that of Velveeta
processed cheese, coining the word Velveetica
to describe it as "not invisible, just boring."

—*Steven McCarthy*

AAAAAAGH!!! Die, Times Roman, die, die, die!!!
—*A posting at www.abisource.com/mailinglists/abiword-
user/01/July/0048.html*

❧69❧

Don't expect good grammar from the citizenry

If you've been paying attention, you've probably noticed that diction, grammar, and punctuation are now of little concern to many of your fellow citizens. It's not uncommon to see "10 items or less" when "10 items or fewer" is correct. Or "childrens'" when "children's" is correct. Or sentences with commas where semicolons should be. Because of inadequate education and indifference, Standard English ain't what it used to be.

Lots of folks see writing errors and nearly have a conniption. After all, *they* make an effort to use language correctly, so why can't everyone? They expect people to understand the importance of Standard English and reel every time it is abused. They expect everyone to follow the rules that ensure clear communication. Sadly, these people are setting themselves up for a lifetime of frustration. Don't be one of them!

Get used to the idea that the bar has been lowered. You can find examples of poor writing in advertisements, newspaper columns, magazine articles, novels, and even scholarly papers. So don't get frustrated—it's out of your hands. But neither should you lower your standards and become part of the problem. You should lead by example and always strive to write well.

Fun activities

Ask people on the street if they know the difference between an
em dash and an en dash.

Edit a sloppy newspaper article with a red pen and mail it to the
writer.

Speculate about how the colon got its name.

Top 10 writing mistakes you're likely to see

1. Missing comma in a series (I saw Fred, Jan and Harold).
2. Interchanging similar-sounding words (The ring fell down the laundry shoot).
3. Pointless redundancy (It was the honest truth).
4. Wordy phrases (Owing to the fact that it's noon, we should leave).
5. Passive voice when inappropriate (The iceberg was rammed by the ship).
6. Dangling modifiers (Entering the museum, the dinosaur looked huge).
7. Unclear references (Beth wanted to go shopping with Kathy, but she was too busy).
8. Plural pronoun with singular noun (When a person drives, they should be careful).
9. Using "etc." without clear meaning (Popular fonts are Times, Palatino, Goudy, etc.).
10. Big words (We must endeavor to ameliorate working conditions).

70

Don't pay your bills by mail

Unless you live in a yurt, are "off the grid," and have no debt, you get bills each month. Electric bill. Phone bill. Mortgage bill. Lots of bills. In fact, it's not uncommon to get a dozen or more bills in a month. And the people who send those bills like to get paid promptly for their products and services. The nerve!

Lots of consumers pay their bills by mail. So for each bill, they write a check, record the payment, stuff the envelope, seal the envelope, affix a stamp and a return address label, and put the envelope into the mailbox. They waste time, effort, and money by sending payments through the postal system. And they live with continual anxiety, wondering from time to time if they remembered to pay every bill. Don't be one of them!

Take advantage of modern technology and have your monthly payments automatically drafted from your checking account. It's great: You pay your bills—always on time—without lifting a finger. So you never have to worry about late payments and the negative effect they might have on your credit rating. And you'll save money on stamps—as much as forty to fifty dollars a year.

Reality check

A single noticeably late payment on an account could put a black mark on your credit report that will cost you higher rates and fees on other accounts. And—yikes—it can stay there and plague you for up to seven years.

Not recommended

PETER: I don't think I'd like another job.

JOANNA: Well, what are you going to do about money and bills and . . .

PETER: You know, I've never really liked paying bills. I don't think I'm gonna do that either.

JOANNA: So what do you wanna do?

PETER: First, I'm gonna take you out to dinner, and then I'm gonna go back to my apartment and watch kung fu. . . .

(Scene from *Office Space,* 20th Century Fox, 1999)

**If you think nobody cares if you're alive,
try missing a couple of car payments.**
—*Earl Wilson*

~71~

Don't let others tell you what's in the Constitution

The United States Constitution is the document that outlines our system of government and guarantees the freedoms we enjoy. It's the most important and valuable document we Americans have.

Unfortunately, a great many U.S. citizens have only a vague idea about what's in their Constitution. They know that the First Amendment guarantees freedom of speech. And they know that some amendment repealed Prohibition. And they know from watching *Law & Order* that the Fifth Amendment is what you "take" if you don't want to incriminate yourself. But beyond that these people depend on others—politicians, pundits, relatives, teachers—to tell them what's in the Constitution. Don't be one of them!

Read the Constitution for yourself. It will take you only about fifteen minutes to read the original document and the Bill of Rights. And while you're at it, read the Declaration of Independence, too. (You can find both documents at www.constitution facts.com.) Find out for yourself what they say (and don't say) about personal rights, government obligations and limitations, and the separation of powers. Then, when someone twists the words in these venerable documents to advance their own agendas, you'll know it.

The Constitution was ratified in 1790, and the Bill of Rights in 1791.

The Declaration of Independence was signed by fifty-six men, including six named William, six named John, one named Caesar, and one named Button.

Constitution quiz

1. Is the phrase "separation of church and state" used?
2. Can Arnold Schwarzenegger become president?
3. Can two states merge to form one state?
4. Is the phrase "right to privacy" used?
5. Is the president required to give a "state of the union" speech to the nation each year?
6. Are Supreme Court justices required to wear black robes?

Answers
6. No.
5. No.
4. No.
3. Yes.
2. No.
1. No.

> The Constitution is not an instrument for the government to restrain the people, it is an instrument for the people to restrain the government—lest it come to dominate our lives and interests.
>
> —*Patrick Henry*

~72~

Don't risk losing important personal items

Your car is important, so you have insurance that enables you to get another car if yours is stolen. And your house and stereo and clothes are important, so you have insurance to replace them if they are destroyed. You prepare for the worst but hope for the best.

Most individuals safeguard the obvious things but leave their most valuable personal possessions unprotected. I'm talking about family photos (and their negatives), personal letters, and other items with sentimental value—things that people truly cherish and would feel an emptiness without. Yet they keep these unique and irreplaceable things in shoe boxes or in file folders where they are vulnerable to destruction by fire or storm or other calamity. Don't be one of them!

Don't risk losing the things that are precious to you. Rent a safe deposit box at your bank just in case the worst happens. In it you can keep important photo negatives, copies of important letters, disks with crucial computer files, and even photos of meaningful physical items (a picture won't be the same as the real thing, but it will be better than nothing).

~73~

Don't tell your dreams to the wrong people

We all have dreams that can guide us to what we believe will be greater achievement or satisfaction or pleasure. Frequently, however, our dreams are out of sync with our reality. For example, a plumber might dream of writing a bestselling novel. Or an overweight woman might dream of running a marathon. Or a shy man might dream of being a public speaker.

Our big dreams are so important to us that we often feel the need to share them with someone. But if you tell your dream to people who don't really care about you and your happiness, you possibly will be told that your dream is ridiculous and not worth pursuing. It might be with an explicit comment, or a dismissive look, or a joke. However it happens, it could be devastating. Many people risk losing their dreams by telling them to the wrong people. Don't be one of them!

Be very selective when you share your dreams. Make sure the people you tell are truly on your side and want you to be happy. Make sure your dream will still be alive and well when the conversation is over. Then you can start turning your dream into specific actions that will take you where you want to go.

74

Don't brag about your gas mileage

Experience tells us, among other things, that (1) not all of our choices are good ones, and (2) we can't control every aspect of our lives. We're not always as informed or objective or lucky as we would like to be when making decisions. Nor is the world a machine that operates consistently and predictably. Most people learn to take it all in stride.

But certain people—you can speculate about the reason—need to believe that they always make the right choices and are always in control. And they spend lots of time and energy trying to convince others of that fact. They're the ones who proudly tell you about their phenomenal gas mileage. "Sure, it's a Huge-mobile with a V-8, but I usually get around twenty-five to thirty miles to the gallon—and that's in the *city*." These people are deluding themselves. Don't be one of them!

Accept the fact that heavier and more powerful vehicles are gas guzzlers. If you drive one, you have nothing to brag about. You get unimpressive mileage. Period. If you want to brag about something, make sure it's something that you, personally, were instrumental in bringing about. And make sure there's more fact than fantasy involved.

☙

Gas mileage figures weren't required to be posted on cars until 1976.

Underinflated tires, dirty air filters, and out-of-tune engines can lower gas mileage significantly.

The ideal mixture in an internal combustion engine is 14.7 parts of air to 1 part of gasoline (by weight).

During the extraordinary chase sequence in *Bullitt,* Steve McQueen's 1968 Mustang GT got very poor gas mileage.

The Honda Insight gets about sixty-one miles per gallon in city driving; the Hummer H2 gets about eight miles per gallon.

I once bought five gallons of gas for one dollar (c. 1970). The place: Spartanburg, South Carolina. The car: a Volkswagen known as "The Red Flame."

Other car things not to brag about

That you "made good time" on a road trip.

That you got a "pretty sweet deal" on your car.

That your car has some expensive option, but that you "rarely use it."

That your car "handles like a dream" in foul weather conditions.

75

Don't fall for the Gambler's Fallacy

If you flip a coin a number of times, you know that because it has two sides, the likelihood of heads and tails coming up is the same over time. So for each flip, the chance of a particular outcome is ½ or 50 percent. The outcome of one flip has absolutely nothing to do with the outcome of the next flip. Over time, and many flips, the heads and tails will even out.

But some people believe that, in the short run, one flip affects the next. For example, they think that flipping five heads in a row makes it highly probable that the next flip will be tails. People who think like this have fallen for "the Gambler's Fallacy"—the idea that, when there is a *fixed* probability, one event affects the next in a predictable way. One of their favorite phrases is: "I think my luck's about to change." Don't be one of them!

Get it through your head that each flip of the coin is an independent event. The same is true of each toss of the dice and each roll of the roulette ball. Sure, you know from practical experience that one outcome can't be repeated forever. But the truth is that there is no way to know, based on recent history, exactly when the outcome will change.

Everyday examples

Although these examples don't represent situations with fixed probabilities, they do illustrate irrational thinking similar to the Gambler's Fallacy:

The price of ConHugeCo's stock has gone down five days in a
    row, so you think it's probably time to buy.
There are lots of planets in the universe, so you believe that
    there must be life out there.
The Bisons have lost several games in a row, so you're confident
    that they're due for a win this week.

Related fallacies

Converse Gambler's Fallacy: Believing that an outcome is less
    likely to occur in the near future because it recently has been
    occurring frequently.
Availability Error: Believing that one outcome is more likely
    because of your tendency to remember that outcome more
    than others (for example, focusing on the few big fish you've
    caught instead of the many tiny ones).

**There is a very easy way to return from a casino
with a small fortune: go there with a large one.**
—Jack Yelton

~76~

Don't use a paper clip to do a binder clip's job

The classic bent-wire paper clip hasn't changed much since it was first manufactured in the late 1800s. And why should it change? It's a simple, elegant, and useful device for holding a few pieces of paper together. Not only are paper clips effective, they also reproduce at a remarkable rate in dark drawers, making it unnecessary ever to buy new ones.

Many people depend exclusively on paper clips for all of their nonpermanent paper-binding needs. It works fine on short stacks of paper, they reason, so why not on thicker stacks as well? So they often push a large paper clip to its limit, forcing it around a stack of papers by twisting it into a grotesque, unnatural form that ruins the clip and can damage the paper. To put it bluntly: they use the wrong tool for the job. Don't be one of them!

Instead, turn to the binder clip when the paper clip clearly is inadequate. Binder clips come in a variety of sizes, with the large ones capable of holding up to 250 sheets of paper. And they also provide a stronger and more secure grip than paper clips. It's true that you can't string them together like you can paper clips. But, on the positive side, they won't leave rust marks on your papers.

Fun activities

While blindfolded, field strip a binder clip, clean it, and reassemble it.

Straighten a paper clip and then try to bend it back to its original shape.

Describe a binder clip so someone who's never seen one would understand what it looks like and how it works.

Link a bunch of paper clips together and try to float them in water (yes, it can be done).

Other uses for a binder clip

stylish money clip
snack bag clip

Other uses for a paper clip

Impromptu lock pick
Inexpensive earrings
Lightning rod for a doll house
Christmas tree decorations
Skewer for small kebobs

The world's biggest paper clip (22.5 feet tall) can be found in Oslo, Norway (in honor of paper clip inventor Johan Vaaler).

The longest paper clip chain made by one person in a twenty-four-hour period is that of Jeanine Van der Meiren (2,688 feet long, containing 22,025 paper clips).

77

Don't use
boring adjectives

No matter how many words you learn, William F. Buckley, Jr., already knows twice as many. That's a scientifically proven fact. But it shouldn't discourage you. Even with the average fifty-thousand-word vocabulary, you still have the capacity for expressing your ideas with clarity, vigor, and style. The right word for any occasion is most likely already in your head, just waiting for the chance to be used.

Lots of people, despite an adequate vocabulary, fall into the habit of using the same adjectives over and over. So they identify some things as "big," or "pretty," or "interesting." And if they need to add more intensity, they say "very big," or "very pretty," or "very interesting." Don't be one of them!

Choose vivid words instead of stretching less appropriate words with qualifiers. For example, instead of "angry," how about "livid" or "furious" or "piqued" or "enraged" or "incensed"? These are not uncommon words. Nor would they be misunderstood by most people. So don't fall into a rut. Add a little zing to your conversations by choosing appropriate and accurate words.

Let's get wordy

Name some other words for:

attractive	bad
difficult	happy
large	great
small	sad
fight	strange
cut	idiot
destroy	fast
good	nice

**One forgets words as one forgets names.
One's vocabulary needs constant fertilizing or it will die.**

—Evelyn Waugh

**I want my vocabulary to have a very large range,
but the words must be alive. *[very large?]***

—James Agee

78

Don't pick movies based on critics' reviews

Hundreds of movies are released each year by major and independent studios despite the risks involved. Why? Because people are willing to pay to see movies. They like to escape to different worlds. They like to root for likable characters and boo despicable characters. They like to be entertained. But with so many movies competing for their attention, how do they choose the ones to watch?

Lots of movie lovers depend heavily on the reviews of movie critics. These people are, I suppose, trying to make an informed and responsible decision. Choosing a movie to watch is, after all, serious business, and they wouldn't want to make a mistake. So when deciding which movies to see, they give great weight to the words of critics. Don't be one of them!

Professional movie critics typically are knowledgeable about the nuances of screenplay structure, story pacing, and dialogue. And they very likely have a more extensive movie-relevant vocabulary than you. And they probably have seen more movies than you ever will see. But can they predict whether you will enjoy a particular movie? Survey says: no. The bottom line is that they merely are expressing their

personal opinions while trying to be entertaining and/or con-
troversial.

Oops

> [*2001: A Space Odyssey*] . . . is so completely absorbed
> in its own problems . . . that it is somewhere between
> hypnotic and immensely boring.
>
> —*Renata Adler,* The New York Times

> [*Star Wars* is] . . . an epic without a dream. . . . Lucas
> has the tone of bad movies down pat. . . .
>
> —The New Yorker

> Alfred Hitchcock, who produced and directed [*Vertigo*] . . . has
> never before indulged in such farfetched nonsense.
>
> —*John McCarten,* The New Yorker

> [*It's a Wonderful Life* is] . . . doggerel masquerading as art.
>
> —*Pauline Kael*

> [*Close Encounters of the Third Kind*] is all flash with no flesh, so if
> you see it, park your disbelief in a snowbank along with your car.
>
> —The Globe and Mail *(Toronto)*

79

Don't wake up
to an alarm

The great thing about a day off is that you can sleep in. On most days, however, you have to get up and get to work or school or the golf course. Leaving your comfortable, quiet bed for the active world isn't very appealing, but it must be done. Some people have the ability to awaken at a particular time each day. But the rest of us need a little help.

Lots of folks use alarm clocks that generate harsh, dissonant, preternatural sounds like buzzes or beeps or pulses. They've always used alarm clocks, which are cheap and functional, so they never consider the alternative. They probably don't like being jolted from their slumber, yet they wake to an alarm day after day. Don't be one of them!

Do you go abruptly from being awake to being asleep? Not bloody likely. Then why go abruptly from being asleep to being awake? It makes no sense. It's much better to ease into wakefulness as pleasant music wafts through the air and into your consciousness. Alarms signal danger and urgency. You really don't need to start your day with that in mind. If you want to get your day off to a good start, wake up to music.

≈80≈

Don't think that failure is the opposite of success

My Webster's dictionary defines *success* as "a favorable termination of a venture." And it defines *failure* as a "lack of success." But does that distinction really make sense? Are success and failure mutually exclusive in the world of practical experience?

Lots of people think they are. They tend to see the world in "either/or" terms. So you either scored the touchdown or you didn't. You either built the bookcase or you didn't. You either graduated from law school or you didn't. These people have accepted the conventional notion that failure is the opposite of success. Don't be one of them!

Realize that success is not an event but a *process,* and that failure is part of that process. Don't believe me? Then consider this: Thomas Edison and his assistants tried six thousand types of filaments before finding one that worked effectively. Were those six thousand attempts failures? No, because they were stepping stones that created a path to the goal. So the next time you think you have failed, consider the possibility that you may have advanced one step closer to your goal.

～81～

Don't eat
canned spinach

According to the all-knowing Food Pyramid, we're supposed to eat lots of vegetables to maintain health (no, ketchup doesn't count). Although fresh veggies are probably most healthful, canned ones are a close second because of the sophistication of modern canning techniques. Many of us rely on canned veggies because of their convenience, quality, and long shelf life. But are they as tasty and appealing?

Most veggies that come in cans are perfectly acceptable to the senses. Corn, beans, peas, and carrots seem to retain most of their flavor and texture during the canning process. But spinach doesn't fare so well. Canned spinach has a mushy texture and unappealing flavor, and usually has a lot of added sodium. Nevertheless, some people insist on eating it. Don't be one of them!

Buy frozen spinach instead. After you zap it for a few minutes in the microwave, you'll have a nutritious side dish that bears little resemblance in taste, color, or flavor to the canned version. (Fresh spinach is good, too, but you have to eat it soon after purchase because the nutrients start to fade quickly.)

True or false?

1. Seventy-five percent of the iron in spinach can be absorbed by the body.
2. Iron is an excellent source of vitamins A and C.
3. Spinach arrived in America in the early 1900s.
4. Spinach doesn't rhyme with anything except Kucinich, the congressman from Ohio.

Answers

4. True.
3. False. It arrived in the early 1800s.
2. True.
1. False. Only 5 percent is absorbed.

I don't like spinach, and I'm glad I don't, because if I liked it I'd eat it, and I just hate it.
—*Clarence Darrow*

The myth about the high iron content in spinach comes from a report of research done in the 1890s by German scientists. They inadvertently misplaced a decimal point, thus making spinach appear to have ten times the iron that it actually has. Sorry, Popeye.

≈**82**≈

Don't say "utilize"
when "use" will do

Alexander Haig, then Secretary of State, once said, "At the moment, we are subsumed in the vortex of criticality." What the heck did he mean? I don't know. But the point is that some people seem to like to use fancy words when simpler words will do just fine. "Use" becomes "utilize." "Payment" becomes "remuneration." "Aid" becomes "facilitate."

While most of us understand that the goal of communication is to be understood, certain people see impressing others as the goal. Each time they speak or write, they hope to demonstrate their great intellect and awe others with their command of the English language. Don't be one of them!

Don't seek the approval of others by using big words. Your ideas will lose their force, and you will be seen as a windbag. Instead, speak and write clearly and directly so people can understand you. Avoid pretentious words, flowery expressions, and jargon. And by all means, avoid unnecessary French or Latin phrases.

Other words not to use (and their less pretentious alternatives)

altercation (fight)
ameliorate (improve)
appellation (name)
cogitate (think)
diminution (decrease)
domicile (home)
impecunious (poor)
lachrymose (tearful)
masticate (chew)
prevarication (lie)
procure (buy)
pulchritude (beauty)
pusillanimous (timid)
salubrious (healthful)
terminate (end)
vociferate (shout)

**Most of our daily conversations draw from
a vocabulary bank of no more than 3000 words . . .**

—Susan Canizares

Verbosity leads to unclear, inarticulate things.

—Dan Quayle

‎❧83❧‎

Don't expect scientific studies
to reveal the truth

Science has brought us many wonderful things. Cures for diseases. Nutritious foods. Cell phones. Unbreakable soda bottles. Using the empirical method—observation, experimentation, and measurement—researchers have forced nature to give up many of her secrets.

Most folks believe that science, with its rigorous methodology, is infallible. So when they hear the latest findings regarding health, the environment, or human development, they accept the new "facts" without question. They take great comfort in the fact that research findings are quantified and analyzed statistically. They think that research provides "proof" for theories. Don't be one of them!

Realize that scientific studies provide *evidence*, not proof (and certainly not "truth"). Individual studies suggest possible answers to questions, but conclusions require that many studies, using many different methods, point in the same direction. Science isn't a means for finding quick and certain facts. It's a slow, methodical process that is prone to missteps. The process is not 100 percent reliable, nor are researchers 100 percent objective.

So it's best to maintain a healthy skepticism each time you hear about the latest "breakthrough" on the evening news.

Potential problems in scientific research

Inadequate sample size
Uncooperative subjects (in the social sciences)
Experimenter bias or incompetence
Tendency to confirm popular theories
Selective reporting

It is a good morning exercise for a research scientist
to discard a pet hypothesis every day before breakfast.

—*Konrad Lorenz*

Science is one thing, wisdom is another. Science
is an edged tool, with which men play like children,
and cut their own fingers.

—*Arthur Eddington*

The great tragedy of Science—the slaying of a beautiful
hypothesis by an ugly fact.

—*Thomas H. Huxley*

There is something fascinating about science.
One gets such wholesale returns of conjecture out
of such a trifling investment of fact.

—*Mark Twain*

~84~

Don't use old-fashioned pot holders

If you eat, you probably cook. And if you cook, you definitely have pot holders. They very likely are made of cloth and are printed with homey images or phrases such as "Home Sweet Home" or "Kiss the Cook." Pot holders like these add warmth and a personal touch to any kitchen. In fact, yours might have been handmade by Grandma.

Many people use these cloth pot holders to remove hot baking dishes full of bubbling-hot food from the oven. Typically, within moments they start to feel the heat transferring to their hands. So they have to move the dish at an unsafe speed toward the nearest trivet and plop it down. And they continue to use these inadequate pot holders day after day to protect themselves from burns. Don't be one of them!

Keep your cloth pot holders for decoration, but use high-tech silicone pot holders for grabbing hot stuff. Silicone is a synthetic rubber that is strong and flexible, resists water and many chemicals, and doesn't support bacteria growth. But, most important, it withstands temperatures to 500 degrees or higher. So update your pot holders and reduce your risk of burns in the kitchen.

✌

The term "silicone" was first coined by the German chemist Friedrich Wohler in 1857.

Silicone polymers were discovered by Frederic Stanley Kipping at the University of Nottingham, England, around 1900. His research formed the basis for the development of synthetic rubber.

Silicone rubber is derived from quartz, rock, or sand.

Silicone, in some form, is used in medical devices, food packages, personal care products, sealants, and, of course, breast implants.

Just in case

If you do happen to burn yourself, you might want to cover the burn with either aloe vera gel or mustard (and let it dry). I've heard that they both relieve the pain and aid healing. I've also heard that covering the burn with a slice of onion helps (but if you've just burned yourself, do you really want to take the time to slice an onion?).

∼85∼

Don't forget the people you meet

How many times have you found yourself in the following situation? You're among a group of strangers, perhaps at a party or a job interview or a meeting. Everything's going fine until the one person you do know decides to introduce you to a few people. Then, suddenly, you're forced into socializing mode. And by the time all of the "Nice to meet yous" and "How are yous" and other greetings are over, the names of those nice folks have, unfortunately, slipped away.

Most people know this is likely to happen, but they never do anything about it. They continually meet people and immediately forget their names. Some are likely to attribute the problem to a "poor memory," and therefore never assume responsibility for the problem. Don't be one of them!

Remember each person's name by immediately forming a *vivid* mental image that associates the new information (the person's name) with something you already know. For example, if it's Rob, see him robbing a bank. If it's Jill, see her walking down a hill with a pail of water. If it's Sandy, see her sunbathing on a beach. If it's Richard, see him saying, "Well, I'm *not* a crook" like another Richard did a few years ago. Got it? It's easy (after a little practice), and it always works. You just have to get into the habit of doing it.

Effective explicit recall depends upon proper elaborative encoding. Unless a name is actively rehearsed or a mnemonic strategy is invoked, recall is likely to be poor.

—*Paul J. Whalen*

If you remember my name, you pay me a subtle compliment; you indicate that I have made an impression on you.

—*Dale Carnegie*

I never forget a face, but in your case I'll be glad to make an exception.

—*Groucho Marx*

I always have trouble remembering three things: faces, names, and—I can't remember what the third thing is.

—*Fred Allen*

~86~

Don't take 11 items to the Express Lane

There are two kinds of people in the world: those who plan their grocery shopping and visit the supermarket once a week, and those who shop whenever they notice they have run out of some things. For the latter group, supermarkets have established the Express Lane, which usually is indicated by a grammatically incorrect sign that reads "10 Items Or Less."*

Lots of shoppers, carrying their little handbaskets, avoid counting what they have for fear of discovering that they are buying eleven or twelve items. That would mean waiting in a "regular" line behind the SuperMoms and their overflowing carts. So they just glance at the contents of their basket and assume they have no more than ten items. Then they head for the Express Lane. Don't be one of them!

Remember that the Express Lane is a privilege, not a right. Those who have provided it can just as easily take it away if you start to take it for granted. So the next time you're tempted to break the rule, consider the consequences. And besides, do you really want to endure the embarrassment of having the cashier say, "Which ten do you want to buy?"

---

*Less refers to size or amount; fewer refers to individual items.

≈87≈

Don't use all of your brain power

Scientists tell us that we use only about 10 percent of our brainpower. And that seems adequate, considering that human minds created the microchip, synthetic rubber, *The Sun Also Rises*, the airplane, Styrofoam, the Brandenburg concertos, kung fu, and the cordless drill.

But there are lots of folks who seem determined to increase their brainpower, so they train their memory with various exercises. And they learn lots of problem-solving techniques. And they read everything they can find. Don't be one of them!

Just imagine how strange things would be if you used all of your brainpower. When you played Scrabble, you'd win by five hundred points every time. When you read a mystery, you'd know whodunit in the first chapter. When you shopped for groceries, you'd know the total before the cashier does. You'd be able to name that tune in one note. You'd know how to set your VCR clock without checking the manual. And you'd understand the meaning of every word William F. Buckley, Jr. ever used. After a while, it wouldn't be much fun. So if you must increase your brain power, stop at 11 percent.

～88～

Don't embrace the $1 coins

The Susan B. Anthony dollar coin was introduced, at great expense to the taxpayers, in 1979. The public didn't like it and didn't use it. So, predictably, the federal government repeated the mistake in 2000, creating—at great expense to the taxpayers—the Sacagawea Golden Dollar. This time, the dollar coin didn't look like a quarter. Big whoop.

These dollar coins have four obvious disadvantages. First, they are heavier than dollar bills. Second, you can't fold them. Third, cashiers look at you funny if you try to use them to pay for stuff. And fourth, they jingle in your pocket, making it virtually impossible for you to sneak up on someone. But some people embrace and use the coins anyway. Don't be one of them!

If you use the coin, you're just rewarding the government for doing pointless things with your hard-earned money. And you're unwittingly moving us toward a slippery slope. Next, the five-dollar coin, then the ten. Then—probably—the paper quarter and the paper half-dollar. Stop the madness before it gets out of hand!

∽

Dollar coins have been issued at various times since 1794.

The smallest dollar coin was one-fourth smaller than today's dime.

The golden dollar is 88.5 percent copper, 6.0 percent zinc, 3.5 percent manganese, and 2.0 percent nickel.

Glenna Goodacre designed the new coin's image of Sacagawea.

Sacagawea was a Shoshone Indian who helped the historic Lewis and Clark expedition in their quest to get really, really lost.

Quiz

Which of the following women were considered for the golden dollar coin?

Emma Lazarus, who wrote the poem that appears on the Statue of Liberty

Mama Cass, singer with The Mamas and the Papas

Phyllis Diller, comedienne

Juliette Gordon Low, founder of the Girl Scouts

Lorena Bobbit, knife expert

Mary Ball Washington, George Washington's mother

Kathleen Maddox, mother of Charles Manson

Answer

Emma Lazarus, Juliette Gordon Low, and Mary Ball Washington were considered. Phyllis Diller was actually in the running until someone realized she wasn't fully dead.

~~89~~

Don't ignore your ideas

What do the polio vaccine, the laptop computer, the Pet Rock, and Viagra all have in common? They all began with an idea in someone's head. At one moment there was nothing, and the next, there was an idea. The first step on a journey had been taken. The process of creation was under way.

People of every age, race, creed, and color get ideas every day. They get ideas while driving, and watching TV, and eating lunch, and taking a shower. And they typically think, "Wouldn't *that* be interesting," or "I wonder if anyone's thought of that," or, "What a great idea." Then most of them immediately go on to some other activity. They let their ideas slip away. Don't be one of them!

These are *your* ideas. Your experience, your goals, your personality, and your desires have created a unique mind that can develop (receive?) unique ideas. They are worthy of consideration simply because they have come into your consciousness. So write down all of your ideas. Then evaluate them critically and decide if they deserve to be brought to life today, or tomorrow, or five years from now. If you don't, who will?

Helpful tip

Make sure you have a notepad handy at all times. Keep one in your pocket or purse, at your desk, by your easy chair, by your bed, in the kitchen, and in your car. Oh, and don't forget to keep pencils handy, too.

The way to get good ideas is to get lots of ideas,
and throw the bad ones away.

—*Linus Pauling*

Many ideas are good for a limited time—not forever.

—*Robert Townsend*

Success is often just an idea away.

—*Frank Tyger*

Don't worry about people stealing your ideas.
If your ideas are any good, you'll have to ram
them down people's throats.

—*Howard Aiken*

For more effective thinking, rotate your ideas every 10,000
thoughts. Creativity involves not only generating new ideas, but
escaping from obsolete ones as well.

—*Roger von Oech*

~90~

Don't look at the keyboard

Typing ability used to be important mostly to secretaries, authors, aspiring authors, and librarians who created the countless little cards that went into card catalogs.* But today, because of our dependence on personal computers, the ability to type is important to everyone. So why do vast numbers of people—including computer users—still feel uneasy at the keyboard?

You know these people. Even though they've been using computers for years, they still "hunt and peck." Before hitting any key, which they've hit in the same location a billion times before, they look at it to make sure it's still there. Only then do they put the appropriate finger into motion. These people have become addicted to peeking. Don't be one of them!

---

*Card catalog: A handsome wooden cabinet that once occupied a central place in all libraries.† Contained in its multitude of drawers were cards that identified all of the books and other items in the library's collection. Using it required no typing skill. In the name of progress, card catalogs have been replaced with unattractive, plastic PCs (which, incidentally, require typing skill to use).

†Library: A building in which quiet people, armed only with pen and paper, did research in the days before the Internet.

Don't let fear of making mistakes at the keyboard keep you from reaching your full human-computer interaction potential. Understand that PCs and Macs aren't typewriters. Whereas typewriters are passive, computers are active. Today's word-processing software can catch most of your spelling and grammar errors. So relax as you type and focus on your writing, not on the keys.

The QWERTY keyboard, so named because of the arrangement of the first six letters, is the one that most of us use. Some people complain that the keys are arranged in a way that makes no sense. And they are correct. Christopher Sholes patented the first practical typewriter, similar to today's models, in 1868. However, the letters were arranged in alphabetical order. This arrangement led to jamming of the type bars when fast typists used the machine. The solution was to slow typing speed by rearranging the keys in a nonalphabetical order. So an associate, James Densmore, devised the QWERTY keyboard with that goal in mind.

> **If my doctor told me I had only six minutes
> to live, I wouldn't brood. I'd type a little faster.**
>
> —*Isaac Asimov*

❧91❧

Don't write indecisively

Good writers know that their primary goal is to present their thoughts so that readers can understand them. If they don't, they fail, no matter what kind of creativity or insight they might demonstrate. So they are careful to choose words that convey ideas without ambiguity. And they don't dilute the power of those words with unnecessary qualifiers.

But lots of folks are timid when they write. They are afraid of appearing too opinionated or too committed to a particular point of view. They want their readers to see them as being reasonable and fair-minded. So they tend to write sentences like these:

I called an ambulance because the injury seemed rather serious.
Learning to play the sonata was a fairly challenging task.
Smedley wasted no time in hiring a somewhat attractive secretary.

Don't be one of them!

Words such as "rather," "fairly," and "somewhat" don't help your readers. In the examples, how is "rather serious" different from "serious?" How does "fairly challenging" compare to "challenging?" And what, exactly, does "somewhat attractive" imply? Using qualifiers such as these weakens the impact of sentences by creating some uncertainty. So give your thoughts increased power by eliminating the unnecessary qualifiers and writing with confidence.

Other warning signs of indecisive writing

Overusing euphemisms
Frequently using the passive voice
Relying on clichés
Running sentences together
Using lazy words (such as "fine," "nice," and "neat")

The difference between the right word and the almost right word is the difference between lightning and a lightning bug.
—*Mark Twain*

Recommended reading

When Good People Write Bad Sentences by Robert W. Harris
On Writing Well by William Zinsser

∽92∼

Don't underestimate the size of the universe

Once upon a time it was believed that what we see in the night sky are lights carried around the Earth in relatively nearby transparent crystal spheres. Over the centuries, thanks to technological advances, the complexity and size and population of the known universe has expanded at a mind-boggling rate. And, to borrow a line from The Carpenters, we've only just begun.

Many of your fellow Earthlings refuse to confront the vastness of the universe. They try to make it manageable by casually using terms like "millions of light years" and "billions of galaxies" and "trillions of stars." They believe that because they can quantify the distances and shapes and masses out there (using without question the numbers provided by physicists), they are dealing with something that really isn't so awe inspiring. Don't be one of them!

Science can help us understand processes and forces and distances. But the universe as a whole remains wondrous, perplexing, and unfathomable. Merely repeating big numbers and scientific terminology won't change that. So the next time you look upward on a clear night, don't let numbers and words limit the universe that you see (and imagine) before you.

How far is far?

In a commercial jet, you can fly from New York to Los Angeles in five hours. At that speed, it would take almost eighteen years to reach the sun. To reach the *nearest* star outside the solar system, you would have to travel for over four million years! (And the most distant stars are *four billion* times as far away!)

How big is big?

Start in New York City (after obtaining the necessary permits) laying Ping-Pong balls in a single file. When will you lay down the one-billionth ball? When you reach Pittsburgh? Indianapolis? Wichita? Los Angeles? In fact, when you reach Los Angeles, you'll just be getting started. You'll have to repeat the process *seven more times* to reach one billion. (If you lay one ball per second, you'll need—hold on to your hat—about thirty-one years to complete the task!)

Can we actually "know" the universe? My God, it's hard
enough finding your way around in Chinatown.

—*Woody Allen*

Recommended reading

One, Two, Three . . . Infinity by George Gamow

93

Don't let the
pessimists get you down

Optimists see the glass as half full; pessimists see it as half empty. Pessimists dwell on problems and expect the worst. They include cynics, defeatists, killjoys, misanthropes, party poopers, sourpusses, wet blankets, and worry warts.

Plenty of people allow themselves to be pulled in by pessimists. They hear warnings of doom and gloom and get frightened. They hear about alarming trends and patterns and become disturbed. And they hear about widespread problems and shortages and become troubled. Don't be one of them!

History shows that things get better, not worse, over time. Problems get solved. Opportunities increase. Knowledge expands. Why? Because human ingenuity, compassion, and curiosity are unlimited. So whenever you hear pessimists talk, keep in mind that they have a *reason* for trying to sell you their negative view of reality. Some want more power, while others want more fame or wealth or control or respect. Also keep in mind that pessimists tend to base their views on incomplete knowledge, using one fact to create a theory or one data point to establish a trend.

❦94❧

Don't keep gloves in your glove compartment

All cars come with a swing-open box called the glove compartment. You probably know that it is designed to hit the knees of the person in the passenger seat when opened. What you might not know is that in the good old days, when seats were vinyl and seat belts were unheard of, the inside of the door had circular depressions where you could put your sodas while eating at a drive-in.

The glove compartment is a handy place to keep a pen, a notepad, sunglasses, emergency cash, a flashlight, and your car registration. No one keeps *gloves* in there, right? Wrong. Some drivers, who apparently take things literally, actually do keep gloves in their glove compartment. Don't be one of them!

Here's why. Imagine you have been in an accident and you're trapped inside your about-to-explode car. The emergency crew comes and pries open the passenger door with the Jaws of Life so they can drag you out to safety. In doing so, the glove compartment pops opens and out drops a pair of gloves. The time they spend laughing at this could mean the difference between life and death—your life, your death. So play it safe. Keep your gloves on the backseat.

∼95∼

Don't fret over
the salt on potato chips

Sodium (salt) is needed by the body to regulate the balance of fluids and to ensure proper conduction of nerve impulses. We need about 1,000 milligrams (mg) each day to maintain health (that's half a teaspoon), and can tolerate up to 2,500. But too much sodium can lead to health problems. That's why many people wisely watch the sodium they consume.

However, some individuals make the mistake of judging the sodium content of foods by their taste. They think, for instance, that potato chips are unhealthy because they taste salty. But in reality, they contain relatively little salt. It just happens to be on the surface where it makes a big impact on the taste buds. These people are focusing on the wrong stuff. Don't be one of them!

If you're going to worry about sodium (and you should), make sure your attention is focused on the real culprits: fast-food and processed foods. These are the real enemies. So find out the salt content of foods you eat. You probably will be stunned at the amount of salt you've been consuming.

Would you like fries with your sodium?

McDonald's Big Mac (1,070 mg)
Wendy's Big Bacon Classic (1,460 mg)
Burger King Whopper (900 mg)
Hardee's Grilled Chicken Sandwich (950 mg)
McDonald's Grilled Chicken Deluxe (1,040 mg)
Arby's Light Roast Turkey Deluxe (1,260 mg)
Subway Chicken or Turkey Sub (6-inch) (1,190 mg)
Taco Bell Burrito Supreme (1,230 mg)
Wendy's Bacon & Cheese baked potato (1,390 mg)

High-sodium processed foods

wiener (420 mg)
barbecue sauce (280 mg/tablespoon)
V8 juice (590 mg/8 ounces)
canned clam chowder (890 mg/serving)
SPAM (790 mg/2 ounces)
frozen pepperoni pizza (810 mg/4 ounces)
instant chicken-flavored noodles (1,480 mg/serving)

A fast-food restaurant salt package contains about 200 mg of
    sodium.
A high salt diet can increase risk for high blood pressure, kidney
    disease, and stroke.
Salt once was used as money: ". . . in Rome . . . the soldier's pay
    was originally salt and the word salary derives from it . . ."
    (from *Plinius Naturalis Historia XXXI*).

96

Don't forget who shot J.R.

Dallas, the soapy CBS drama that followed the exploits of the ruthless J.R. Ewing, was the number-one show on TV in 1980. Part of the reason was the March 20th episode in which someone sneaked into J.R.'s office and—gasp!—shot him. Twice. For the next eight months, J.R. fever swept the nation. J.R. merchandise flew off the shelves, Larry Hagman became the highest paid actor on TV, and everyone speculated about the shooter. When, on November 21, Kristin Shepard finally was revealed to be the culprit, it was the most widely watched show in TV history.

It was memorable. And yet lots of people don't remember. Sure, they remember *Dallas,* but not the details. If you ask them, "Who shot J.R.?" they're likely to say something like, "Oh, I think it was Sue Ellen, or maybe that—oh, what was her name? Hmm, I guess it really doesn't matter." Don't be one of them!

Of course it matters. The "Kristin shot J.R." episode released the great burden of doubt that we, as a nation, had carried for eight long months. Then we all were able to take a deep breath and get on with our lives. That night, we didn't just see a one-hour episode. We witnessed a unique television event. So don't forget who shot J.R. It's too important.

Things in "Dallas" you can forget

The impostor Jock.
The "Bobby was dead for a whole year but it was a dream"
  story.
All scenes with Dusty Farlow.

"Dallas" quiz

Who said:
1. "Sue Ellen, you're a drunk, a tramp, and an unfit mother."
2. "Nobody gives you power. Real power is something you
   TAKE!"
3. "Never get caught in bed with a live man or a dead woman."
4. "Ray, get me the shotgun out of the hall closet."
5. "I am Tokapa! I AM TOKAPA!"
6. "You BASTARD!"

Answers

6. Sue Ellen (although we would have accepted any
   female character.)
5. Jock
4. Miss Ellie
3. J.R.
2. Jock
1. J.R.

97

Don't become a measurement chauvinist

Here in the U.S. of A., we have a system of weights and measures that was derived from the British Imperial System. So we use feet, pounds, gallons, and acres. In various other places, they have the International System, or metric system, and rely on meters, kilograms, liters, and hectares. Our system is based on the numbers 4, 12, 16, and 5,280, among others. The metric system is based exclusively on the number 10.

Each system has its proponents and critics. Advocates on one side will point out that the American system makes it easy to divide things into fourths and eighths. Advocates on the other side will point out that the metric system makes it easy to divide things into tenths. These people argue passionately about which measurement system is superior. Don't be one of them!

Realize that the world is a big place and there's room for both measurement systems. Let's be objective. Both allow equally precise measurement, right? Neither is convenient in all situations, right? So can't we all just get along? We've made strides in eliminating racism, sexism, and ageism. Now let's address the next great challenge: measurementism.

Questions to ponder

Why isn't there a metric day, hour, and minute?
Do they have inchworms in countries using the metric system?
How does one identify a "2×4" in metric-speak?
What, exactly, is a yottameter?
Do they allow Ray Bradbury's novel *Fahrenheit 451* in metric
    countries?
If we went metric, what would we call The Daytona 500?

> **Drugs have taught an entire generation of American
> kids the metric system.**
>
> —*P. J. O'Rourke*

> **If God had intended for us to use the metric system,
> He would have given us ten fingers.**
>
> —*Author unknown*

> **. . . the metric system did not really catch on in the States,
> unless you count the increasing popularity
> of the nine-millimeter bullet.**
>
> —*Dave Barry*

98

Don't use boring
postage stamps

Standard-issue postage stamps are the ones you get by default at the post office. And they're the ones you can buy from vending machines and at supermarkets. There's no doubt that they are functional—they will get your mail to its destination. But they usually are boring.

Many people buy these stamps over and over again without a second thought. They mail letter after letter with the same kind of stamp, causing their mail to look exactly like the mail of millions of their fellow citizens. Don't be one of them!

Instead, buy and use commemorative stamps. These interesting stamps portray people, subjects, and events that are important parts of the "American experience." Buying commemoratives takes a little more effort: You have to coax a postal employee to drag out the Big Book o' Stamps. But using them will give you pleasure and give your mail a touch of distinction. And the recipients of your letters will enjoy a pleasant aesthetic moment that otherwise would not occur.

In 1893 Postmaster General John Wanamaker issued the nation's first commemorative postage stamps. Congress passed a resolution condemning the "unnecessary" stamps.

The Elvis stamp was issued on January 8, 1993. Since then, more than 500 million have been sold.

Top 10 most popular stamps

1. Elvis (1993)
2. Wildflowers (1992)
3. Rock and Roll (1993)
4. Civil War (1995)
5. Legends of the West (1994)
6. Marilyn Monroe (1995)
7. Bugs Bunny (1997)
8. Summer Olympics (1992)
9. The World of Dinosaurs (1997)
10. Centennial Olympic Games (1996)

Fun activities

Celebrate National Stamp Collecting Month (it's October).

Create your own special stamps. You can do it at www.photo .stamps.com. At this Web site, you can upload a photo—of yourself or your dog, perhaps—and have it placed on actual postage stamps. And it's all sanctioned by the U.S. Postal Service. Way cool!

99

Don't become a wine expert

Wine has been called "the nectar of the gods." But most of us just call it "something to drink occasionally with a meal." We know that it's either red or white. Red goes with meat and white goes with chicken. I'm not sure what goes with shrimp and grits.

But some individuals believe that there's much, much more to it than that. They believe that an "educated palate" is essential to happiness and self-esteem. So they go to a great deal of time and effort, and spend quite a lot of money, to become wine experts (also known as oenophiles or wine geeks). They become obsessed with many arcane things concerning the taste, color, and smell of wine. Don't be one of them!

Enjoy wine if you want to. And by all means sample different kinds of wine. But resist the urge to become a wine expert. Otherwise, the seven-dollar Chianti from Food Lion that you now thoroughly enjoy with your Friday night spaghetti will become unpalatable.

Most annoying words oenophiles use to describe wine

amusing
muscular
good humored
intense
obscure
pretentious
impudent

> When I find someone I respect writing about an edgy, nervous wine that dithered in the glass, I cringe. When I hear someone I don't respect talking about an austere, unforgiving wine, I turn a bit austere and unforgiving myself. . . . You can call a wine red and dry and strong and pleasant. After that, watch out. . . ."
>
> —*Kingsley Amis*

> I rather like bad wine . . . one gets so bored with good wine.
>
> —*Benjamin Disraeli*

Don't try this at home

BOND: Unusually fine Solera. '51, I believe.

M: There is no year for sherry, Double-O-Seven.

BOND: I was referring to the original vintage on which the sherry is based, sir. 1851. Unmistakable.

MUNGER: Precisely.

(Scene from *Diamonds Are Forever,* United Artists, 1971)

❧ 100 ❧

Don't confuse Randy Quaid with Dennis Quaid

Randy Quaid and Dennis Quaid are brothers. They have the same last name. They have the same vocation—acting. And they have the same educational background—less than four years of college. But that's where the similarity between the two ends. If you've been paying attention during the last two decades, you've no doubt noticed that they have different looks, different talents, different voices, and different careers.

Nevertheless, some people seem to have trouble keeping the Quaid boys straight. These people will, quite innocently, say things like, "Boy, that Randy Quaid sure has a nice head of hair," or, "Dennis Quaid was *so* funny in *Christmas Vacation*." These people are very confused. Don't be one of them!

Don't just lump the Quaids together. They deserve better than that. They're not interchangeable, you know. So take the time to get to know these veteran actors and their bodies of work. Watch their movies. Learn about their lives. Do the research. There's really no shortcut.

Side-by-side comparison

RANDY QUAID	DENNIS QUAID
bad hair	good hair
funny	not funny
born in October	born in April
originally from Houston	originally from Houston
once played Lyndon Johnson	once played Jerry Lee Lewis
is two inches taller than Dennis	is two inches shorter than Randy
middle name is Rudy	middle name is William
never was married to Meg Ryan	once was married to Meg Ryan

Representative work

Randy Quaid as Cousin Eddie (*National Lampoon's Christmas Vacation*): "He's cute ain't he? Only problem is, he's got a little bit a Mississippi Leg Hound in him. If the mood catches him right, he'll grab your leg and just go to town. You don't want him around if you're wearing short pants, if you know what I mean. Word of warning though, if he does lay into you, it's best to just let him finish."

Dennis Quaid as Remy McSwain (The Big Easy): "If I can't have you, can I at least have my gator?"

> I could never hold a job for more than three months,
> which works out well because that's
> how long a movie shoots.
>
> —*Dennis Quaid*

~101~

Don't make a list of 101 unusual things to do before you die

Life is a cabaret. Seize the day. Life is short. Today is the first day of the rest of your life. Yada yada. Most of us hear these adages over and over again without taking much notice. But some people become concerned about the quality of their lives and decide they must "live life to the fullest" by doing unusual and risky things. And to help, they create long to-do lists to stay motivated.

And what kinds of things do they put on their lists? Have sex in an airplane bathroom. Milk a cow. Bungee jump. Get arrested. For these types of adventures they put unnecessary stress on their bank accounts, their health, their career success, and their relationships. And as time passes, they become more and more frustrated because they find they aren't accumulating check marks fast enough on their to-do lists. Don't be one of them!

By all means have some adventures. And continually stretch your mind and body. But realize that fulfillment most often comes from just living your life with creativity, patience, and resolve. When you learn to value everyday experiences and successes, you won't feel the need to spend a lifetime trying to redefine what living is all about. And you won't even need a list!

Better ideas

Make a long list of things you've already done (and survived).

Vicariously experience interesting things from your La-Z-Boy by reading books and watching movies.

Fun activities

Each time you avoid engaging in a potentially expensive, dangerous, or embarrassing activity, treat yourself to a high-carb meal.

Come up with more descriptive names for risky activities. For example, "running with the bulls" could become "running with the fools," and "bungee jumping" could become "bungee plummeting."

Document each triumph of self-preservation and common sense. For example: Where were you when you decided not to skydive? How did it feel? Were you alone or with others? Was alcohol involved?

> You will never be happy if you continue
> to search for what happiness consists of.
>
> —*Albert Camus*

> It is while you are patiently toiling at the little tasks
> of life that the meaning and shape of the great
> whole of life dawn on you.
>
> —*Phillips Brooks*